*Sunset*

# Beachcombers' Guide
## to the Pacific Coast

*By the Sunset editorial staff*

*Book editor: Bob Thompson*

*LANE BOOKS · MENLO PARK, CALIFORNIA*

# Acknowledgments

The cover photograph by Robert Cox leaves as much to a pleased imagination as the sea itself does. The scene could be near LaJolla, or near Mendocino, or even close to LaPush. It is not. It is near Pescadero, south of San Francisco. The girls could be examining a fossil, an agate, or an unwilling sand crab. They are not. They turned up a piece of sand-scoured wood that looked a little like Winnie the Pooh.

The drawings spaced through the book are by Carol Johnston, done in the same spirit of good humored inquiry as that employed by the girls on the cover during their long afternoon's hike.

The information in the text comes from Sunset, the Magazine of Western Living, and Sunset Books, from biology handbooks and histories, and from state departments of fish and game, state highway departments, state parks departments, and local chambers of commerce from Port Angeles, Wash., to San Diego, Calif.

# Photo credits

**Barry Anderson:** 9 (top), 39 (l.), 103. **William Aplin:** 7 (r.), 12, 19, 20, 21. **Robert L. Berme:** 73 (low). **Ernest Braun:** 7 (l.), 9 (low), 10 (top l.), 17 (top l., low l.), 23. **Wynn Bullock:** 36 (l.). **Tom Burns, Jr.:** 77 (r.). **Don Chapman:** 83. **Clyde Childress:** 32 (top). **Glenn Christiansen:** 15, 17 (r.), 18 (top), 30, 78. **Herbert Clarke:** 88 (low l., low r.). **Frances Coleberd:** 36 (r.), 49, 50 (low). **Bob Cox:** 44 (l.). **Dick Dawson:** 10 (top r.), 26, 27 (r.), 32 (low), 33, 35 (l.), 44 (top r.), 56, 57, 58. **Madison Devlin:** 55. **Glenn Dixon:** 44 (low r.). **L. O. Gocean:** 42, 46 (l.), 64, 65 (top l., top r.), 76 (l.), 81 (low), 82 (r.), 86 (l.), 91 (top l., top r.). **Greensmith:** 8. **Mike Hayden:** 27 (l.), 39 (r.), 40, 53 (r.). **Walter Houk:** 37 (l.). **Jim Hosmer:** 82 (l.). **Yuki King:** 22. **Dorothy Krell:** 41 (top). **Ted Lau:** 11 (low). **Martin Litton:** 25, 65 (low), 104 (top). **Jim Martin:** 62 (r.). **Ken Metzler:** 76 (r.), 77 (l.). **David Muench:** 16. **Josef Muench:** 79. **Tom Myers:** 28, 47, 61, 112. **Oregon State Highway Commission:** 70, 81 (top), 89, 91 (low r.). **Phil Palmer:** 54. **Hugh Paradise:** 95, 99. **Ralph Poole:** 10 (center, low l.), 18 (low), 37 (center, r.). **Redwood Empire Association:** 62 (l.). **Hal Roth:** 50 (top), 51. **Edward Sievers:** 11 (top). **Bob and Ira Spring:** 67, 71 (r.), 97 (r.), 102 (low). **Hugh Stratford:** 86 (r.). **Frank Thomas:** 29. **Harolyn Thompson:** 35 (r.), 41 (low), 43, 45, 71 (l.), 73 (top, center), 81 (center), 97 (l.), 98, 107. **Eric Wahleen:** 106 (r.). **Darrow Watt:** 46 (r.), 109, 110. **Elton Welke:** 93, 106 (l.). **Emory Wells:** 69. **Alain Whitman:** 53 (l.). **Woody Williams:** 10 (low l.). **Doug Wilson:** 88 (top l., top r., low center). **Steven C. Wilson:** 96, 101, 102 (top), 104 (low), 105. **George Woo:** 5.

Sixth Printing July 1970

# Contents

# A note of introduction

In the southwest corner of the United States, the shore is almost entirely urban. The seawater washing it is warm enough to make swimming a pleasant exercise, and the climate is an embracing one the year around. European exploration and settlement led to the complete expulsion of the original, Indian inhabitants from the region. Now the local economy is dominated by space industries, and San Diego and its satellite towns are a sophisticated center for tourism. The traffic on seaside highways is dense and rapid.

In the far northwest corner of the United States, the shore is largely primitive. The seawater washing it is cold enough to keep sane men out of it unless they are wearing diving gear, and the climate is a bracing one the year around. European exploration and settlement led to very little change and never amounted to much in numbers. The original, Indian inhabitants are still the most numerous inhabitants of the region. The local economy is dominated by fishing, augmented by some lumbering, and Neah Bay (without satellite towns) is a rough-hewn center for tourism. There are no seaside highways.

In between there are greater and lesser population centers, rockier and sandier stretches of coast, but mainly more moderate examples of one extreme or the other.

The sea and the edge of the sea in this scientific age still hold enough mystery to draw curious men. They also hold enough known attractions—fish, shellfish, driftwood, semi-precious stones, surfing waves, whatever—to attract all kinds of people who are not so much curious as they are in need of a day of outdoor exercise, or outdoor relaxation.

In this diversity is the greatest attraction of the sea. It has some aspect for everyman. This book tries to present enough information about each of the publicly accessible beaches between San Diego and Cape Flattery to help steer vacationers or weekend-trip takers to places they might enjoy. It pays very little attention to anything not subject to the spray of waves, except to give general road directions and some idea of available accommodations in each region.

The sea always changes and never changes, on a scale that should not throw the text of this guide out of date soon. Accommodations change on a scale that makes them hard to describe. With some maps, there is an address of a chamber of commerce that maintains printed lists of accommodations. All chambers of commerce are helpful in this regard, and with information about other facilities or activities. Another helpful note: Most libraries have extensive collections of telephone books and yellow pages, which can be informative.

Another sort of fact subject to frequent change is game law for fish, shellfish, and even inedible creatures from tidepools. Limits, license requirements, fees, seasons, reserves—all of these change from year to year. Following are addresses for fish and game departments of the coast states, each of which will send booklets summarizing regulations (plus some special pamphlets on individual sportfish or shellfish).

California Department of Fish and Game, 722 Capitol Avenue, Sacramento, 95811.

Oregon Fish Commission, 307 State Office Building, Portland, 97201.

Washington State Department of Fisheries, 115 General Administration Building, Olympia, 98502.

This book notes shoreside camping areas in brief. But the best all-around guide to camping anywhere in the western states is the *Sunset Campsite Directory*.

# CALIFORNIA COAST

# San Diego, the southwest corner

European exploration of this coast began at San Diego with a Spaniard named Cabrillo, and the first European settlement followed directly. The region remembers the particularly Spanish nature of its birth, and preserves it with care. About the only place the heritage does not show strongly in the architecture is the shore.

In compensation, the air and water temperature have a Mediterranean quality, and the place names are Spanish with a few exceptions.

The Mediterranean warmth of the seawater makes it a pleasure to use. It is not the bathtub of the Bahamas, but a pleasantly brisk solution for swimming, body surfing, surfing, skin diving, or surf fishing. Because of this and because two sheltered bays make it possible to water ski or dawdle about in small boats, the shore is much used.

Because the air is as pleasantly warm as the water, millions of visitors come every year to share the place with the people who live there. The city and towns and their beaches are crowded from July through September, and fairly populous from March through November. The hotels and motels are always equal to the numbers of visitors, although a late-arriving visitor will find his choice limited in summer.

The best months for warm and sunny skies and warm water are July through September. The water temperatures range in the mid-60s and the maximum air temperatures average 73 or 74°. From November to the end of February is the rainy season and the time of coldest water (56°), but the clear days are sparkling clear and fresh, and the days following storms are the best ones drift hunters get all year.

## The City bays and beaches

In populous San Diego, the U.S. Navy requires considerable shoreline for its military needs, and vacationers and townsfolk want room to relax on clean, sandy beaches washed by warm Pacific waters. The fancy scrollwork of the urban shore provides ample space for both.

### IN THE HARBOR

The protected waters of San Diego Bay suit themselves ideally to naval and maritime purposes. The bulk of the harbor shore is lined with piers both military and civil.

**Sportfishing piers** are in the commercial basin to the east of a causeway connecting Shelter Island to the shore. Garrison and Fenelon Streets lead to the piers from the extension of North Harbor Drive. Charter boat trips go for half days to the kelp beds off Point Loma and LaJolla. Full day excursions go to the Mexican Los Coronados islands 18 miles south. The Mexican trips include a license as part of the fee. Anglers in California waters must purchase a state license separately.

The quarry in either case includes albacore, bluefin tuna, barracuda, marlin, bonita, and (king of local sportfish) the yellowtail, which last is related to the eastern amberjack.

Reservations a day in advance are a wise precaution.

**Shelter Island,** a onetime sandbar, is the base of private yacht club activity in the bay, and has as ancillary pleasures to that a number of fine restaurants. Most of this is in the sheltered cove to the west of the causeway. On its bay-facing side, Shelter Island has a public boat launch, a launching pad for water skiers, a 350-foot municipal fishing pier (rock cod, bonito, sea trout, flounder halibut, and sea bass with no license required on the pier), and a beach with fire rings and other amenities for sunbathing picnickers.

Byron Street runs along the causeway from the extension of North Harbor Drive (Scott Street) to the island beach.

*SHORESIDE CAMPING: None. SHORESIDE ACCOMMODATIONS: On Shelter Island, Mission Bay, at Mission Beach, Pacific Beach, LaJolla. Write San Diego Visitor and Convention Bureau, 924 Second Avenue, San Diego, 92101, for list.*

*Summer sun-lovers* at Windansea—Winter walker at Silver Strand

**Harbor Island,** parallel to Shelter Island and also man-made, is more for boats than beaches.

## CORONADO AND ITS SILVER STRAND

The outer side of San Diego Bay supports on a low-lying, sandy peninsula a naval air station, a pleasant resort community, and a day-use state park of some national fame.

A hump-backed bridge connects downtown San Diego with Coronado. It has replaced the old ferry forever, saving commuters four minutes and five cents per crossing. On the Coronado side, the visiting beachcomber has immediate access to either bay or ocean beaches.

**Glorietta Bay** is the small boat harbor of Coronado, and has a public launching ramp in addition to moorage. A municipal golf course adjoins the harbor, and adjoining it is a public bathing beach that extends to the south city limits. Warm water and gentle waves make the swimming safe and pleasant at this beach, as at other bay beaches. There is one matter of concern, especially in spring when the crowds first begin to come out, and that is the sting ray. The animals naturally inhabit the bay beaches, and it always takes a few weeks of heavy human activity to discourage the main numbers of them from lurking about the wading zone. A few will persist in returning each evening, to retreat only when a new day's crowd arrives.

Novices at swimming in this region should know to avoid pioneering a new stretch of sandy shoal, and also that the sting only seems fatal as it produces soreness and swelling in the affected part.

**Central Beach,** the main ocean beach in Coronado, runs north from the point where the skinny neck of the peninsula swells into North Island. It begins almost opposite Glorietta Bay. The shore is wide, sandy, and gently sloping.

Lifeguards patrol during the daylight areas. No fires are permitted. It is strictly for swimming and sunbathing. Ocean Boulevard parallels the back shore for the entire mile.

**North Beach** adjacent to Central Beach and extending to the boundary of North Island Naval Air Station, is beset by rip-currents and is thereby not a good place to swim. It has a few fire rings for picnickers, or chilled surf fishermen.

**Silver Strand State Park,** of sufficient natural beauty and thoughtful enough human development to rank as one of America's fine day-use parks, occupies almost the entirety of the long sand spit that connects North Island to the mainland at Imperial Beach.

On its ocean side, the beach face is steep, and silvered with fragments of countless tiny shells. There is some clamming, although the beds have been rather thoroughly depleted over the years. Surf bathing is limited to those swimmers or waders sturdy enough to withstand the rapid backrush of waves on a sharp slope. Surf fishing is fair, mainly for sea bass, corbina, croaker, and perch. The grunion run at this beach is notably good.

The sand is dotted by nearly 400 fire rings for picnickers, primary summer users of Silver Strand, which has parking space for 2,000 automobiles, and which has a climate almost unfailingly beneficent for such pursuits.

In winter, when the water cools just enough to thin out the population of swimmers, a cool and windy day will cast up a bit of drift on an almost deserted beach. A hardy beachcomber out with the dawn tide can come close to the kind of solitude his counterpart in hardier climes to the north will expect on any day.

The bay side of Silver Strand (pedestrian underpasses cross beneath busy State Highway 75) is the swimmers' side and the water skiers'. (The skiers launch from Glorietta Bay and ride parallel to the park shore.)

# Whale watching

California gray whales cruise close to the Southern California coast each winter on the way from summer patrols in the Bering Sea to their calving grounds in the Gulf of California, a 6000 mile migration.

Watching the 40 to 50-foot, ton-a-foot creatures burrow along at a steady rate of four knots is a stirring experience, one that thousands of people repeat often.

The season begins with a few scattered pods (whales travel in pods, but are not as alike as peas) passing Point Conception late in November. It reaches a crescendo at mid-January, then trails away in February. In mid-January, 70 to 80 whales a day of the herd of 7,000 pass Point Loma in San Diego. (The return route, in spring, is well offshore.)

Whales, like dolphins and other sea-borne mammals, are credited with high intelligence. Some scientists think whales can navigate by visual reference to shore points. If they are not the frolicsome showmen that dolphins are, the whales at least tolerate ogling mankind and go on about their business with relaxed assurance.

Typically, *Rhachinaectes glaucus* executes a regular diving-breathing sequence. From three to five successive spouts usually signals a dive that will cover about 1,000 feet of horizontal distance in about three or four minutes. More spouts signal a longer dive. The spout is vapor exhaled from the animal's huge lungs as he huffs and puffs the same way a human swimmer does to prepare for a deep dive. The signal is useful to whale-watchers as a clue to where to look next.

The best watching station on land is Point Cabrillo National Monument on Point Loma in San Diego. During the season, rangers give illustrated lectures on the natural history of the whale. The exposed location of the old light station there allows an observer to track a single whale for an hour or more, from north horizon to south.

The lecture schedule is hourly from 11 a.m. to 4 p.m. Saturdays and Sundays only, and the site is an amphitheater.

A good pair of field glasses is a whale-watcher's best friend at this vantage, or at Point Dume, the Palos Verdes peninsula, Laguna Beach or La Jolla. Less predictable vantage points are all exposed headlands south of San Francisco.

Charter boat services in San Diego, Mission Bay, and Long Beach suspend fishing trips on highlight days during the season and put out for half days of close-up watching. The schedules are the whales' schedules, so it is necessary to call the sport-fishing piers day to day to find out when trips will be made. The fares generally range around $2.50 a trip for adults, half-fare for children under 12.

**Imperial Beach,** on the ocean shore just south of Silver Strand, attracts surfers, picnickers, and sunbathers for the most part. Swimming is good, and lifeguards patrol the sandy beach. Here, and at other San Diego beaches, surfing goes on in reserved zones marked by flags. Swimmers are prohibited from the surfing zones, and vice versa. Still another attraction is a public fishing pier.

## POINT LOMA TO LaJOLLA

Rocks, reefs and coves carve the ocean front of north San Diego into a series of short beaches, and at the same time set up wave and current conditions so drastically various that a distance of only a few feet can move a visitor from a good swimming area to a small paradise for surfers, to a current-swept cauldron where only skindivers safely venture.

**Cabrillo National Monument,** on the tip of Point Loma as it overlaps North Island to form the narrow mouth of San Diego Bay, marks the point where Spanish explorer Juan Rodriguez Cabrillo was the first European to set foot on California soil. He landed on or near Ballast Point in 1542. He liked the place and said so in his report to the king. In the 1960's, Cabrillo National Monument attracts two million visitors a year. Most of them come to visit the "Old Spanish Lighthouse," named with a cheerful inexactness reflective of the mixed cultural heritage of the city. It was neither Spanish nor even Mexican by origin, but the workaday product of an 1855 appropriation by the U.S. Congress. It ceased to be a working light after a new one was built closer to the water in 1891, and its main function now is to provide visitors with a sparkling panorama of mountains, city, bay, ocean, off-shore islands, ships, and (from November to February) gray whales.

The old lantern room serves as the prime platform and is the best dryland vantage on the coast for whale watching.

The monument and light station are in the midst of military reservations. The only road intersects with Canon Street in San Diego, but since it is part of a sign-guided tour of the city, there's no trouble finding it.

**Ocean Beach,** at the foot of Santa Monica Avenue and just south of the San Diego River flood channel, has a diverse character. At the south end where rocks crop out into the water is a reserved zone for surfboarders. A rip current surges along the shore within the area. About 300 yards up the beach begins the safe, lifeguard-protected swimming area. Offshore skin divers can pick up halibut, spiny lobsters, and an occasional abalone. (Many local divers prefer to work off Sunset Cliffs, to the south.) A new fishing pier (no license) was scheduled to open in spring, 1966. Grunion runs are consistent.

There are about 20 fire rings for picnickers.

**New Mission Beach,** on the north spit of Mission Bay, has beaches on both the bay and ocean sides of the spit. It is highly civilized area. Picnickers have fire rings every 20 yards. Rental stalls have every sort of beach equipment. An amusement park occupies the center ground.

Swimming, body surfing, and surf fishing are all pursued along the beach, which ranges south from the foot of Ventura.

**Old Mission Beach,** at the foot of Santa Clara Place, has fire rings and lifeguard service, and no other services. Wide, sandy, with gradually deepening water, it is a pleasing beach for people who can prepare elsewhere, and arrive self-contained. Grunion run on this beach most years.

**South Pacific Beach** at the foot of Grand Avenue has swimming conditions suited to small children. There are fire rings every 20 yards, along with restrooms, showers.

**North Pacific Beach** at the foot of Diamond Street off Mission Boulevard, has a variety of water conditions. Near the bluff, surfing is good. The most suitable area for swimmers is north of Crystal Pier (rip-currents make things tough right around the pier). A few fire rings and the usual sanitary facilities are near a grass lawn behind the beach itself. Pier fishermen can use this pier for a slight fee, and must have a valid California ocean fishing license. (The fishing is good; the license is required because the pier is operated by private interests.) Grunion hit the shore most years.

**Bird Rock,** off Dolphin Place, is not a park beach. It has no facilities, but does have two points of interest. The rocky area harbors a number of good tidepools between two small coves of sand and beyond each. Second, an unusual underwater topography just to the north causes waves to come in fast and sideways to the shore. The beach and its waves are called The Freaks.

**Windansea Beach,** legendary in the lexicon of the surfer and pleasant for swimmers to boot, is at the foot of Rosemont. The surfing reserve is at the north end of the beach, where breakers spill toward shore at heights of six feet most days, and get bigger on occasion. This beach is the home ground of a number of California's international class competitors, and they rate it with Hawaii's best.

A less heroic majority swims at the south end of the beach. Lifeguards patrol during daylight hours.

**Casa Pool** (Scripps Pool) is protected by a curving breakwater that tames the surf, making this beach one of the safest in the area for children who are still in small sizes. Skindivers like to work the deep waters around the breakwater. No fires are permitted on this beach at all. It is on Coast Boulevard just south of Jenner Street.

**LaJolla Cove,** on Cave Street at the north end of Scripps Park, is a small cove with a small beach, with calm clear water that attracts both veteran and novice skindivers, who swim along the reef in company of Garibaldi, bass, and other rockfish. It is a small area and is at capacity early every day.

**LaJolla Shores,** in North LaJolla, reached by Calle Frescota from La Jolla Shores Drive, extends from Scripps Pier south to La Jolla Beach and Tennis Club (private). Long and flat, with a wide expanse of white sand, the water deepens gradually. This is a family beach, one of the safest in the area for ocean swimming. Pismo clams can endure in the general conditions, and a few remain to be dug. Skin divers spearfish for halibut just offshore. The surf kicks up a bit to the north, at the end of the seawall, and especially at the Scripps Institution pier.

Of beach amenities, there are 30 fire rings, restrooms, changing rooms, and lifeguards the year around.

Night beach parties are a fixed part of the local scene.

## MISSION BAY AQUATIC PARK

Mission Bay in an inspired moment of civic planning was retrieved from rubbishy bogginess and set up as a sparkling

*Look close*, there's a whale tail at far left

*Sitting* and waiting is a pleasure of bank fishing

*LaJolla Beach* is popular for beach fire dinners        *LaJolla Cove* attracts skin divers and lookers-on

*Sea turtle* at Scripps; Black abalone and sea hare at Scripps and in nearby tidepools

center for all kinds of recreation and relaxation, most of it aquatic. Large portions of the shore are set aside for bank fishermen. Water skiers have launching pads here and there about. Swimming beaches dot the bay margin. An oceanarium and amusement park are in the bay and next to it. Charter services run deep sea fishing expeditions. Restaurants adjoin the boat harbors and motel and hotel complexes.

## SCRIPPS INSTITUTION

A visit to the Thomas Wayland Vaughan Aquarium-Museum at Scripps Institution of Oceanography (a part of the University of California) is one of the easiest ways in the world to go back to school.

A great many of the mysteries the ocean turns up to the view of beachwalkers have their explanations in the museum, which has model exhibits of the workings of tides and currents, and live exhibits of animals common to the southern California coast.

Charts and models explain how sand beaches form, how waves begin and travel until they pound into surf, how tides and currents travel their regular routes across the great oceanic expanses, and other matters having to do with the effects of water on beaches.

Live exhibits range from deep water animals to more familiar intertidal creatures. Starfish, sea anemones, sea pansies, nudibranchs, and hermit crabs are some of the creatures of the tide zone a visitor can observe here. Spiny lobsters, crabs, Garibaldi, perch and small octopi are creatures of habits that draw long attention from observers. Sharks, yellowtails, sardines, moray eels, kelp-fish, cabezon, and lumbering green sea turtles augment a cast of thousands. The show is non-stop, but visiting hours are limited to 9 a.m. to 5 p.m. weekdays and 10 a.m. to 6 p.m. weekends and holidays. Admission to the museum is free, but in the spirit of the times it costs a small fee to park a car at the adjacent lot.

A sign on La Jolla Shores Boulevard north of the town points the way to the aquarium.

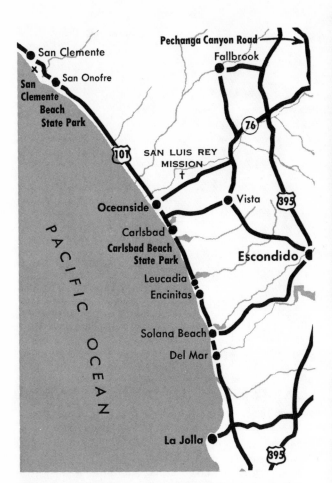

**Glider pilot** *puts on a show at Torrey Pines*

**A Torrey pine** *in state park of the same name*

*SHORESIDE CAMPING: South Carlsbad State Park (226 units). SHORESIDE ACCOMMODATIONS: Imperial Beach, Del Mar, Solana Beach, Carlsbad, Oceanside. Write San Diego Visitor and Convention Bureau, 924 Second Avenue, San Diego, 92101, for list.*

# The County coastline

North of the city of San Diego, the county coast rolls along for another 40 miles, starting with the rugged preserve of Torrey Pines State Park, proceeding through a string of shore-oriented vacation villages, and winding up in the battle-pocked preserve of the U.S. Marines, Camp Pendleton. It is a haven of surfers, sunbathers, surf fishermen, and Hedon himself could find no fault with the weather.

## TORREY PINES STATE PARK

Golfers, glider pilots, naturalists and fossil hunters all find special interest in this park, which further is one of the best in the state for family outings, short hikes, and lolling about on sand beaches.

The golfers choose between two fine courses, both part of the San Diego municipal system and not technically a part of the state park. Golfers whose skill fails them create an overlapping use of the facilities.

Glider pilots get up airspeed by means of a winch, which casts them adrift at the edge of a bluff which rises to 200 feet above sea level. The sailplanes turn along the bluffs to ride upwelling drafts of the westerlies. Unless the breezes fail, the pilot returns to land on the mesa top. Periodically, somebody arrives at the edge of the bluff during a lull, and has to land on the beach far below. The gliderport is just off U.S. 101 three miles north of LaJolla, on the south extremity of the park.

In the park proper is the preserve which protects the only stand of Torrey pines in the nation. The wind-sculpted trees, some of them with large amounts of their root systems exposed on the bluff faces, number about 2,500. Theirs has been an epic battle to survive against the strong ocean winds, but survive they have, all twisted and gnarled, and a rare sight even to veteran viewers of the Monterey cypress in its last stand farther north. The main access point to the mesa-top preserve is at the golf courses. From the

*Torrey Pines Beach at the foot of sandstone bluffs, south of Del Mar*

parking area at the ranger station trails strike out along the bluffs to several viewpoints. Only one, Flat Rock Trail, leads to the beach.

Easier and more extensive beach access is at the south end of that stretch of U.S. 101 that comes close to sea level south of the town of Del Mar. There a sign marks the turnoff to the west. Parking is permitted along the shoulder of the turnoff road, which ends at a ranger station.

As for the beach, it is broad and sandy below the bluffs, which project into the high tide surf here and there. Wise beachwalkers get a local tide table before they set out on long hikes on the shore, which is four and-a-half miles long in the park.

The surf along the park beaches is rough most of the summer to the point that swimming requires vigorous exertion. It abates in September and October. The mildest currents occur along the beach where U.S. 101 stays close to sea level. The worst currents occur near Sorrento Bridge.

The picnic area is up on the bluffs, and no open fires are permitted. Picnickers can bring portable stoves.

## RESORT TOWNS AND PARKS

North of Torrey Pines mesa, there begins a long string of state beach parks, most of which border resort towns. The towns, and in some cases San Diego County, maintain beaches to supplement the state-owned areas. The net result is that the great part of the shore is publicly accessible. The subsequent description will include the entire lot.

**Del Mar,** a community known mainly for the presence of the horse racing plant of the same name, maintains three beach areas. The one at the foot of 15th Street has swimming, surf fishing, body surfing, and rather well-regarded surfing. Summer lifeguards, restrooms, and a concessionaire are welcome amenities. At the foot of 25th Street, the beach has swimming, surf fishing, and body surfing. There are summer lifeguards, but no restrooms. The parking is not exactly capacious at either of these, but Solana Beach has fairly sizeable lots in addition to on-street parking. This beach, a mile and a half north of 25th Street and 22 miles north of San Diego, has swimming and offshore fishing near kelp beds. It is the best organized of the three for picnics, with tables, fire rings, a concession, and restrooms.

**Tide Park Beach,** a county beach one mile north of Solano, offers skindivers some excellent spearfishing opportunities. Lobsters and abalone inhabit the rocky shore, too. The beach has fire rings, but the rest of the amenities are back in Solano Beach town. Lifeguards watch swimmers in summer.

**San Elijo Beach State Park,** the most southerly of the state beach units, is a mile north of Solano Beach, in Cardiff. The area is scheduled to undergo a remodeling in the near future, which will make of it a camping park. In the meantime, it is a rallying ground for surfers. The swimming is good, too. There is a lifeguard in summer, and the beach has fire rings, restrooms, and too little parking space.

**Moonlight Beach State Park** in spite of its name bespeaking romantic evenings with the surf whispering sweet nothings, is a park given over to violent exercise. It has tennis and volleyball courts, a baseball diamond and other such paraphernalia. It has picnic tables, wood stoves, a rental shop for beach gear, and a children's playground. The swimming and body surfing are good, and there is a reserved area for surfers. Lifeguards patrol the year around.

The park is at Encinitas, 26 miles north of San Diego.

**Ponto Beach State Park,** in Leucadia at the foot of Neptune Avenue, is just a beach, at the foot of a long flight of stairs (the sandstone bluffs that attain their greatest heights at Torrey Pines recur all along). Jeep-borne lifeguards patrol in summer, and a restroom is open only in summer. A small parking area is the only parking permitted.

**South Carlsbad Beach State Park** got a new name along with its considerable face lifting. Visitors with previous experience would know it as La Costa. Visitors with a good deal of previous experience would know it as Gypsy Camp. The old, primitive campsites are gone. In their place are 226 tent and trailer sites spaced out along the high bluff, overlooking a wide, clean beach. This beach is among the safest of the beaches in the county for ocean swimming, and it is one of the few that permits open fires (on the shore, not on the bluff).

Lifeguard service is summer only at the beach, which is at Leucadia, 34 miles north of San Diego.

**Carlsbad Beach State Park,** 4,000 foot of ocean front at the foot of Tamarack Street in the town of Carlsbad, also has safe swimming. There are fire rings for picnickers. Agua Hedionda Lagoon, behind the beach, has boating and waterskiing facilities. There is some surf fishing, mainly for corvina.

The town of Carlsbad built its early fame around the similarity of its water to that of the original Karlsbad in what has become Czechoslovakia, but was at the time Bohemia. These days, mineral springs are not the sure fire lure they used to be, but Carlsbad goes merrily on attracting thousands of visitors a year to its ocean beach, springs, lagoon, and poinsettia fields.

**Oceanside,** just a mile north and the last civilian outpost before Camp Pendleton, is a good deal like Carlsbad, but bigger. The city beach extends four miles from end to end, and a 1,900-foot public fishing pier protrudes from it while a small boat basin recedes from it.

The town goes back a long way, as California beach resorts measure time. There are photographs extant, of young women promenading in the sand in 1887, wearing costumes that would guarantee their owners' drowning if they ever got wet. The original fishing pier was operating in 1910, although it did not at that time have tram service to its outer reaches, and did not draw anything like its current annual crowd of 225,000 fishermen.

Charter boats operate from the small boat basin, going out for the same range of fish as their downcoast counter-parts in San Diego: albacore, bluefin tuna, barracuda, marlin, bonito, and yellowtail.

The main fame of the beach is as a competition class surfing area. The annual invitational meet here has stature among surfers just one rung below the international championships. As is the case with most good surfing areas, the same beach offers good body surfing and swimming in adjacent areas where underwater topography changes the nature of incoming waves just a bit. Lifeguards are on hand summers only.

Skin divers spearfish and explore an offshore reef.

The beach has fire rings and restrooms, and the business district is close at hand for other needs.

Beyond Oceanside, the shore is closed to the public in Camp Pendleton. The Marines practice amphibious assaults from time to time, and conduct other, dryer exercises along the shore area.

**San Onofre,** on the north side of Camp Pendleton and right next San Clemente (Orange County), has a beach of two fames. It is great for surfers and for surf fishermen.

## In pursuit of the grunion

Almost every grunion story written in this century starts out by saying that the grunion is indeed real, and not a vast practical joke like snipe hunts, Charley Noble, or left-handed monkey wrenches.

It has been beyond the capacity of a skeptical people to believe that a man could go out by the side of the sea and scoop up fish with his bare hands, on a night predicted well in advance. However, experience has taught that it is indeed possible, that it happens every year on a few favored beaches in Southern California.

*Leuresthes tenuis,* a seven-inch, silver-sided fish swims ashore to spawn much like a smelt, in the summer months from March through September. The schools always come in the second, third, and fourth nights following the full moon, in a three hour period following the high tide.

A regular fishing license is required to take the fish, and the only way they may be taken is with the bare hands. No nets may be used, and game laws forbid digging a trough in the sand to trap the fish as waves recede. The uniform of the grunion hunter is tennis shoes (no socks), cut-off pants, and a sweatshirt plus a complete change of clothes handy in the car. The method is to build a warm beach fire, then to patrol a likely beach looking for flashing bits of silver in the surf line.

It helps to have a flashlight during the search, but it is a matter of faith that the beam should never be shined out over the water. Hunters should stay above each advancing wave.

There is no limit, but April and May are closed months.

The famed beaches are Silver Strand, Pacific, La Jolla Shores and Del Mar in San Diego; Doheny Beach State Park in Orange County, and Carpinteria near Santa Barbara. Less famous but look-alike beaches may produce good runs, too.

# Los Angeles and its far reaches

Los Angeles grows and spreads daily into the hills north and east and southeast. There are almost nine million residents in the area if you include not only metropolitan Los Angeles but all of its many environs.

As is true with San Diego and Santa Barbara, Los Angeles enjoys the benefits of warm air and warm ocean water all summer. The huge population makes full use of the sea as a coolant when the summer heat builds. The water temperature is 67° from July until fall. The air temperature at Santa Monica hits an average maximum of about 75° then, while Pasadena is another 10 degrees hotter. At Newport, the air temperature stays in the low 70's. Winters, the water cools to 56°, the air cools to 63°, and violent waves batter some of the shore towns.

Thousands of summer visitors crowd the parks around Santa Monica Bay and a similar number strike out for Orange County—go for swimming, fishing, shore fishing, and picnicking and sunning on the shore. In winter, the surfers and shore fishermen continue their pursuits, and are joined by clammers (the red tides make clams poisonous most summers), drift hunters, and beach hikers. Los Angeles fishermen benefit from a series of reefs (the work of the State Department of Fish and Game) made of old automobiles, streetcars, and anything else that will sink to make a home for fish on an otherwise unsheltered ocean floor.

The shore is mainly urban, rimmed with piers and parks and behind them with businesses and homes. Even in winter it is hard to feel alone and distant from the city in any of the sandy shores, but amazingly this city has a few miles of craggy shore for the loner.

## Palos Verdes Peninsula

Several millenia ago, Palos Verdes Peninsula was an island in fact. In contemporary Los Angeles it is connected to the mainland, but continues to be a refuge apart for the urban-weary Angeleno. Its seaward side is so steep that, from the beach, it hides everything but rocks on one side and the sea on the other.

For all of that, it has an educative amusement of national prominence on the same shore.

### MARINELAND OF THE PACIFIC

Three-fourths of a ton of whale bursting straight up out of the water makes an impressive sight. When the show is handy in an amphitheater that uses the Pacific Ocean as a backdrop, it can hardly be matched for its first-handedness and convenience.

The prime purpose of Marineland is entertainment, but the oceanarium has a remarkable collection of hundreds of varieties of sealife, and it invites lingering looks between the scheduled performances.

There are three separate shows, which run serially in repeating cycles from 11 a.m. to 5 p.m. in winter and 7 p.m. in summer. The longest, 30 minutes, is called a "seal circus and porpoise games." Its featured performers are California sea lions and Atlantic bottle nose dolphins, who go by the mis-nomers because circuses and sea lore have caused it to be popularly held that sea lions are seals and dolphins are porpoises. A second show is the feeding by a diver of 2,000 fish (100 species), in a tank with windows that look in on the underwater mess facilities. The eating habits of the varied lot (sawfish, sharks, rays, and the common creatures fishermen catch) are the points of interest. The third show is brief but bulky. It is whales cavorting in a very large tank.

Because the sea lion can rotate his hind flippers, he can be trained to unlikely feats of balance, ball-playing, and general acrobatics. In addition, he will sing, and dive from a high board (which, after all, is only a pale imitation of the dives he will do naturally from high cliffs), and it is this sort of stuff that makes the show.

The incredible member of the cast is the Atlantic bottle-nose dolphin. Dolphins occupy the serious attention of scientists who are curious to know more about the sonar navigation system dolphins use, about their proven language capacity, and about the ultimate mental capacity of a brain as complex as man's, but larger. Along with their intellectual capacities, Atlantic bottle-nose dolphins have fully articulated necks which allow them to balance and throw balls and other objects with uncanny accuracy.

Other mammals on display at Marineland include: the

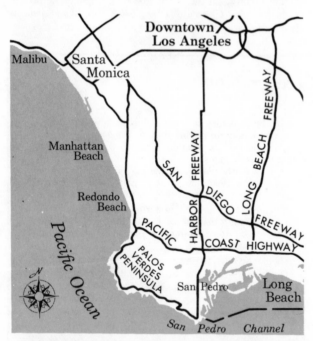

*SHORESIDE CAMPING: Leo Carrillo State Park (140 units) is 16 miles west of Malibu. SHORESIDE ACCOMMODATIONS: Redondo Beach, Manhattan Beach, Santa Monica, Malibu. No single lists available.*

*The inhospitable rocky Palos Verde shore gives way north of Bluff Cove to sandy Santa Monica Bay*

Pacific pilot whale, false killer whale, common dolphin, striped dolphin, Pacific bottle nose dolphin, harbor seal, and Pacific walrus (which last is a lovable beast of such overwhelmingly comic mien that it does not even undergo training).

The ticket to get in costs $2.50 for adults, teen-agers go for 90 cents (until they pass 17), and sub-teens get in for 50 cents. The price includes the shows, but it is another $1.50 for an offshore boat ride (75 and 50 cents for youngsters as above) that lasts an hour as it takes in the Palos Verdes shoreline plus whatever happens to swim past. Parking is free.

The complex of buildings is off Palos Verdes Drive at Long Point, just about the mid-point of the peninsula.

## PALOS VERDES BEACHES

These beaches refute the general concept of a Los Angeles beach. Instead of being long and sandy, they are a series of short, rocky coves in which swimming is dangerous and sunbathing next to impossible.

Tidepool browsers, rock fishermen, skin divers and wave watchers struggle with the difficult terrain to get at unusually good grounds for each of these pursuits.

Topography made the place a suitable site for smugglers and whalers in the nineteenth century, and no doubt attracted a fair share of entrepreneurs during Prohibition. That same topography makes a running series of half day visits the best way to see what marks the contemporary scene. High tides lap against the cliffs. Low tides uncover narrow pathways of rock that connect some of the parts together. Generally speaking, a visitor can roam no more than one beach per tide.

In the best of circumstances, there is no way to walk the entire shore. Tidal bores balk beach walkers at several points and are impassable at any tide.

**Point Vicente** is just west of Marineland. A short distance east of the lighthouse is a graded path leading down the bluffs from a parking area. Point Vicente Light is reached by a spur road off Palos Verdes Drive West. The station is open to visitors from 1 to 4 p.m. only on Tuesdays and Thursdays.

**Resort Point,** more than a mile north of the light, lies below a loop road west of Palos Verdes Drive. The south end of the loop is marked "Via Caleta" and the north end "Paseo Lunado." From it, one access path leads down to a tightly curving cove south of the point. Another, more northerly path drops down into Lunada Bay, the arc of which can be walked all the way to Palos Verdes Point and the disintegrating wreckage of the freighter *Dominator*, and beyond.

North of the loop road noted above, another leads to yet another access path. The south end is marked "Cloyden Road" and the north end "Paseo del Mar." This stretch of beach faces the sea full on, and provides some dramatic wave action when winter waves sweep ashore from storms in the north Pacific. But most of the stirring surf piles in from the south, on southwest facing beaches, because the offshore islands offer a better track for waves bound up from the tropics.

**Flat Rock Point** and Bluff Cove to the south of it mark the northern terminus of tidepooling country. An access path drops down to the rocky shore on the south side of the point.

**Torrance Beach Park** actually belongs more to Santa Monica Bay than to the peninsula beaches. The broad strip of sand that is the margin of Santa Monica Bay ends at Malaga Cove. The park has a full range of facilities for sunbathers, swimmers, and picnickers.

None of the beaches within Palos Verdes Estates (Resort Point to Torrance Beach Park) can be used for picnics. Fires are forbidden along the peninsula, as is overnight

# Two kinds of shorefishing

*Surf fisherman at Malibu*

Along the southern California coast, there are two kinds of fishing to be done from the shore, and they are very different from each other.

Surf fishermen traditionally have been a solitary lot, content to doze beside a pole or two, waiting for some action to get going. There are too many of them now for much solitude south of Point Conception, but it is still a calm way to spend a day of no regrets, catch anything or not.

Surf fishing has something elemental as part of its appeal. Tackle is the only expense, and it does not cost much. Often it can be rented $2 or $3 a day. The annual license fee is $3, and the fishing is year-around whenever the weather is good enough.

The name surf fishing expands to cover both open beach fishing and shallow water fishing in bays.

Three fish are the primary quarry.

Barred surfperch is number one in numbers in southern California. It is found most often along sandy beaches, and tends to congregate in the troughs between sand bars in surf zones. Typically, a fish weighs a bit less than three pounds. The barred surfperch will strike the year around at sand crabs, bloodworms, mussels, and commercial sugared cut-mackerel. The best beaches are sandy ones between Point Conception and Point Mugu.

California corbina, a bottom fish belonging to the croaker family, inhabits the bottom near sandy beaches and in shallow bays from Point Conception to Baja California. San Onofre has a great reputation for producing this fish, which can be taken all year, but seems more readily caught from July through September. Softshell sand crabs are a favorite bait.

Spotfin croaker has the same range as the corbina, but is most common south of Los Angeles harbor. The best runs are in late summer, and the best place to cast is for the trough just outside the breaker line. Baits that work are marine worms, clams, and mussels.

Just for variety, an occasional staghorn sculpin or shovelnose guitarfish will take the bait, as will a diamond turbot or any of several rays—the first two outside and the latter in bays.

Most anglers gather bait on the spot. Sand crabs bury themselves an inch or two below the sand near the surf line of a changing tide. Marine worms and mussels inhabit rocks of tidepools at the ends of sandy beaches.

A novice looking for equipment will need an 8 to 12-foot Calcutta cane, split bamboo, or glass surf rod (the longer the rod the longer the casting range), and a conventional reel with room for 250 feet of line. Most surf fishermen prefer short-shanked No. 2 to No. 6 hooks with four feet of 12-pound-test leader and six ounces or less of weight. A newcomer to the sport should ask a good tackle shop clerk about rigging this gear.

Rockfishing (and pier fishing) is another matter altogether. These fish live in deep water, stirred perhaps in passing among rocks, but not breaking in waves.

Some of the commonest of the fish are rockfish (a specific kind of fish as well as a kind of fishing), ling cod, scorpion fish, greenling (sea trout), cabezon, and sculpins in variety. Sometimes sole, flounder, or halibut turn up at the end of the line.

The cabezon, sculpins, and rockfish are in general a weird lot to see. The cabezon, for example, has stout spines above each eye that give an appearance of beetle brows. The scaleless body is wrinkled and mottled with brown, tan, red, gray, green, and yellow. It weighs up to 30 pounds, measuring as many as 30 inches in length. It tends to live near the mouths of streams, and is good eating (the roe is poisonous) in spite of the bluish tinge of its flesh.

Rocky shelfs that drop into deep water, jetties, and fishing piers are all good spots for most of these fish. Boats anchored near offshore kelp beds are another chance.

*Playful dolphins at Marineland delight young and old alike*

camping. Except in the park, drinking water is nowhere available.

East of Marineland, the scramble along the shore is tougher than it is north of there because access is less regular and also because the several tidal bores occur in this segment.

**Portuguese Point** cannot be rounded because of tidal bores, although some of Abalone Cove can be explored beneath the overseeing presence of the Wayfarers' Chapel.

**Inspiration Point,** south across a narrow cove, is similarly beset by impassable channels and caves. Southeast beyond it is Portuguese Bend, the area where a number of homes have slipped their moorings in earth slides.

**Royal Palms Beach Park,** off Paseo del Mar (the extension of Western Avenue), is a match for Torrance Beach Park when it comes to picnic and other facilities. It offers one of the few places to swim on the south coast of the peninsula—with a lifeguard on duty in the summer.

**Point Fermin Park** takes up the last few hundred yards of shore before Palos Verdes Peninsula turns to cup the harbors at San Pedro and Long Beach. Most of it sits atop the high bluff, giving viewers long looks across the point itself and out to sea, or back to the harbor. The picnic areas and other facilities are on that pleasantly verdant mesa. But wide, paved paths lead down to the shore, which has tidepools with sea hares, starfish, anemones, sea urchins, small octopi, black abalones, barnacles, mussels, and tube worms. All of these tidepools have been picked often enough that they can ill afford to lose more of their populations to the merely curious.

Whites Point, west of Point Fermin Park, is a site of considerable interest to rockhounds and archaeologists. Marine fossils turn up on the shore, or can be quarried out of the bluffs, which are here formed of diatomaceous earth (the same silicified algae skeletons that filter swimming pool water). Also, concretions—great round millstones by appearance—can be found on this beach. A dirt, pedestrians-only road leads to the shore from the Paseo del Mar near its intersection with Western Avenue. (Malaga Cove has some diatomaceous outcroppings near the old school, and Cabrillo Beach just inside the south tip of the peninsula has yet others.)

*Point Vicente Light is the most modern on this coast*

*Seagull roost: Grounded freighter* Dominator

A venerable lighthouse crowns Point Fermin, and beckons to the historically interested. But it isn't open for any reason to tourists.

**Cabrillo Beach** lies just around the tip of Point Fermin from Point Fermin Beach Park, inside and outside the long, long breakwater that protects Los Angeles and Long Beach harbors. It has a swimming area and picnic facilities, but its distinguishing feature is a marine museum.

No admission is charged to the museum, which has both live and model displays of sea creatures along with a range of exhibits having to do with the human history of the region. One of its much-used services is the publication of a series of pamphlets explaining how to conduct a number of shoreside activities, including tidepool exploring and shell collecting. The museum is at the west end of the breakwater (3720 Stephen M. White Drive), and can be reached via Pacific Avenue from the Harbor Freeway.

The beach, which has a boat launch, can be intensely crowded on weekends, but even then the rock fisherman willing to work his way well out on the breakwater can find plenty of elbow room.

# The Los Angeles Harbors

There are two big ports in the Los Angeles area: Port of Long Beach (the first to be developed) and Port of Los Angeles. The city fathers of Los Angeles caused the latter to be built (starting in 1899) so they would not be dependent upon another municipal government for deepwater port facilities. Port of Los Angeles includes the Terminal Island, San Pedro, and Wilmington districts.

## PORT OF LOS ANGELES

This is industrial harbor. Except for Cabrillo Beach (noted above) and the breakwater fishing, there is little shoreside activity for beachcombers.

Every year on a weekend late in September, the commercial fishermen deck their craft with flowers and parade the harbor in the Fisherman's Fiesta. At other times in the year, visitors can watch everyday wharf activities such as net mending, loading the catches ashore, and related tasks.

As part of a harbor improvement program, there has been developed a commercial complex called Ports of Call Village, in the San Pedro District. It has restaurants, import shops, harbor tour boats, and nautical memorabilia of every size from marlin-spikes up to the ancient San Francisco Bay ferry *Sierra Nevada*.

Sport fishermen who like to get to the open sea for big fish can find party or charter boats at piers at the foot of 6th Street and at 22nd Street.

Terminal Island is one of the main wharf areas for deepwater ships. It is joined to the mainland by the high-level Vincent Thomas Bridge (toll: 25 cents). Terminal Island smells mightily of petroleum most of the time, but there is an impressive array of ships to see.

The departure point for the channel steamer that goes forth each day to Catalina Island, from May to October, is located in the San Pedro district, right beneath the west end of the Vincent Thomas Bridge.

## PORT OF LONG BEACH

Long Beach is important as a naval base, a major port, a manufacturing center, and a resort and recreation area. It has plenty of inland attractions, but the main lure for salt water types is a seven mile arc of white sand, all of it open to swimmers (lifeguards every few hundred feet) and sunbathers (the beach is 500 feet deep). The Belmont Fishing Pier protrudes from the approximate center of this beach, between Redondo Avenue and Park Avenue.

The west end of the beach lies approximately in line with the terminus of the Long Beach Freeway, and the east end of it is a sizable yacht basin. The whole beach is protected by the breakwater offshore, so its waters are calm and current free except at the extreme east end.

Off toward the west end, a mile-long carnival area called Nu-Pike rambles along Ocean Boulevard. Nu-Pike features the standard array of rides, side shows, shooting galleries, stand-up diners, restaurants, curio shops, and penny arcades.

# Orange County's Coast

Orange County's character does not resolve readily. In its northeast quarter it is both industrial and the location of Disneyland. Irvine Ranch is the middle of it, and very little developed to this point. The southeast quarter is mainly dry and untenable hill country. But the coast is pretty much all of a piece. It is a summer resort capital of this populous part of the world. The north end teems rather more than the south.

## BEACH TOWNS AND YACHT HARBORS

Seal Beach abuts the Orange County line, which is by and large synonymous with the Long Beach south city limit at the edge of the sea. The stretch of shore from this point south almost to Huntington Beach has, on the east side of the highway, a considerable presence of petroleum. Applications of modern technology to the wells and other facilities have enabled the beach towns and parks to continue serving the needs of a sun-loving populace with no greater inconvenience than an odor of petroleum in the air.

**Seal Beach** is a beach town in the full sense of the word. So is **Sunset Beach,** next door on the south. U.S. 101 courses along just behind the rim of sand, lined on either side with refreshment stands and places that offer any kind of beach apparel or gear for sale or rent.

**Bolsa Chica Beach State Park,** south of Sunset Beach, is an extension of the general shore characteristic, which is a 300 to 360-foot wide strand of sand adjacent to the highway. The beach has circles of concrete set every few yards, the fire rings that are common to almost all park beaches in the region, and restrooms.

Otherwise, it has lifeguards as do the town beaches to the north of it, and summer crowds that tax its capacity on every fair day.

**Huntington Beach State Park,** next beach to the south, is something of a monument to the capacity of urban people to be tidy. The beach is generally less wide than Bolsa Chica by a few yards. It is two miles long, and its margins are a parking lot at the inshore edge of the sand, and the ocean wherever the tideline happens to be at the

*Dana Cove is popular with tidepoolers, skin divers*

SHORESIDE CAMPING: *San Clemente State Park (48 units, 56 trailer units); Doheny Beach State Park (115 units).* SHORESIDE ACCOMMODATIONS: *San Clemente, Laguna Beach, Balboa, Newport, Huntington Beach, Long Beach. No single lists available.*

instant. Between the two are two long, parallel rows of fire rings, more than 500 of them, and between those rows of rings is a line of refuse cans. The beach is spotlessly clean every morning, even though the fire rings blaze long after sundown on most nights, but especially Saturday.

Concessioners sell or rent gear for those who do not bring their own. Lifeguards are on duty at a beach which has some brisk longshore currents at times.

The south end of the park is the flood control levee of the Santa Ana River, a good place to fish when the weather kicks up a bit.

The town of Huntington Beach, a mile north of the park, has a municipal beach with the usual concessions and lifeguard service. It is not developed for picnics. Rather, it has a municipal pier for fishermen, striking out to sea from the foot of Main Street (4th Street in the number system).

**Newport Beach,** owing to the presence of Newport Bay and its attendant fleet of sand bar islands, offers considerable variety. It is, basically, a center for well-to-do small boat owners. On an average summer weekend, some 4,000 craft bob at their moorings in Newport Bay (while hordes of their brethren come to rest around Catalina's harbor).

The ocean side of Newport Beach is a long, skinny, south-stretching sand spit, the tip of which is Balboa. Both towns provide lifeguard services for their beaches, and both have plenty of small businesses along Ocean Front to serve the needs of swimmers, sunbathers, and pier fishermen. There are two piers. Newport Beach's is west of the intersection of Balboa Boulevard with Newport Boulevard (each street is a main thoroughfare leading west from the Coast Highway, State 1). Balboa's is at the foot of Main Street.

The inner side of the spit, which cradles Lower Newport Bay, is mainly lined with yacht clubs and other private developments.

There is a large park within the bay. Just south of the bridge crossing the upper bay arm, on the east side of the Coast Highway, is a park. Within it is a commercial enterprise called Newport Dunes, which offers dozens of dolled up ways to go swimming in the warm, quiet waters of a small lagoon. After a small entry fee, there are prices on the rental of boats or other flotation gear, and games courts.

There are rock cockles in the gravelly mud of the upper bay, which is part of the Irvine Ranch and destined for future development, and the fishing is fairly productive from boats in the bay.

**Corona del Mar Beach Park** occupies the south side of the bay mouth, and resembles the rest of these beaches in all particulars. It can be reached by turning west off the Coast Highway on any street in Corona del Mar between Orchid and Iris Avenues, and the other names are all as flowery as those two.

## THE SOUTHERN SEGMENT

The Irvine Ranch properties control a considerable stretch of shore between Corona del Mar and Laguna Beach, the next town south. It is a breathing spell during which the

*Waiting for turbot in Newport Bay*

*Safe wading in calm Newport Bay*

topography begins to change from low, lagoon-backed shoreside to a continuing rank of steep bluffs.

**Laguna Beach** maintains a municipal beach much like the others at the north end of this sunny county. It is, in brief, a cheerful mob scene of the kind that goes on at every accessible bit of ocean sand anywhere around the Los Angeles basin.

**Dana Cove Beach State Park** is crowded, too, but by shore and pier fishermen, skin divers, and tidepoolers. Its evolution has proceeded from the time Richard Henry Dana knew it as the cliff over which cow-hides were thrown to waiting traders (see references to Point San Juan in *Two Years Before the Mast*), to a lonely cove in which abalone hunters poked among the rocks, then to a park. The narrow footpath worn by those long-gone abalone hunters became the base of the road down which dozens of cars now roll, carrying people to the fishing pier (no license required; bait hut on the end), or to the beach where surfing is fair to good. Rock fishing from a riprap breakwater along one side of a big parking area requires a license. The swimming is not especially inviting on a rocky beach, but divers find plenty of invertebrates along the rocky bottom.

Turn off the Coast Highway at Blue Lantern Street.

*Tunnels lead from beach to beach at Carrillo*

*Christmas Day sunbathing at Laguna*

*Rock cockle clammers at Malibu Beach*

**Doheny Beach State Park** just south of Dana Cove, is the first of two camping parks. The campsites are atop a bluff, near the highway. Below, 6,500 feet of shore are divided into two zones, one for swimmers, and one for surf fishermen (the usual corbina, spotfin croaker, and barred surfperch plus some turbot). This beach has a fair grunion run, among its other allures.

**Capistrano Beach** lies just south, an adjunct to the old mission town. Just south of town, State 1 reunites with U.S. 101, which latter runs well inland from Los Angeles to this point.

**San Clemente Beach State Park** is similar to Doheny in that the campsites are atop a bluff, overlooking the sea. It is, however, a bit more graciously spacious as a camping park. The park is just west of the town of the same name. In addition to swimming and surf fishing, this park offers to skin divers good hunting for spiny lobsters and abalone.

The campsites sit right out on the edge of the bluff, with panoramic views of the sea whenever the summer fog is not ashore. (An odd chance causes a short length of coast from Capistrano to a point well into Camp Pendleton to have more fog than any other part of the shore south of Los Angeles.) Established foot paths lead down the bluffs to the beaches, and should be used. Extemporaneous routes usually lead to some kind of calamity.

# Santa Monica Bay

Santa Monica Bay swoops in a shallow, 20-mile arc from Redondo Beach on the south to Santa Monica. In that distance, it is entirely urban behind the shore, and entirely sandy upon it. North of Santa Monica, the coastline takes a decided westerly bent, the population thins out rapidly, and the shore starts getting broken and rocky.

## THE LOS ANGELES BEACHES

There is not much to choose between the five segments of Los Angeles Beaches State Park that fall along the populous shore of this long bay. All are administered by the county or municipal governments involved. All are given over to day use (one estimate has it that 40 million visitors a year come out to surf, fish, swim, picnic, and visit the amusement piers at the parks and their adjacent city beaches).

*Always open,* the Venice fishing pier

**Redondo Beach State Park,** the most southerly of the lot, is at the city of Redondo Beach, and its shore is one of the most exposed on the bay. It has pier and barge fishing, and rental boats are available. Lifeguards patrol the shore. Other facilities include dressing rooms, picnic tables, snack bars, and restaurants.

**Hermosa Beach,** just north, has a municipal pier at the foot of logically named Pier Avenue, off the Coast Highway a few blocks south of Artesia Avenue. It is much like others in the region, with a bait and tackle shop, restrooms, and a snack bar for the comfort of anglers.

**Manhattan Beach State Park** has a fishing pier just north of the one at Hermosa Beach. And like Redondo Beach, it has picnic tables, snack bars, and lifeguards. A children's playground adds another note of enjoyment for the young who use it and the elders who relax while their children busy themselves at such harmless play.

**Dockweiler Beach State Park,** next north in the line, sits beneath the takeoff pattern of Los Angeles International Airport. For one reason or another, it is seldom as crowded as its neighbors to either side. It is not because the beach itself is less attractive. The swimming is good, the surfing fair for relative newcomers to the sport, and there are lifeguards. It stretches south from the city of Venice, and is somewhat remote from restaurants and other commercial establishments, at least as a matter of local comparison.

The once-picturesque canals of Venice are behind the park beach area.

**Venice** has a beach and municipal fishing pier at the foot of Washington Street. The pier is thoughtfully designed and organized for round-the-clock fishing. It has bays at short intervals to expand its perimeter (it being about 400 yards long), and its concrete pilings are centered beneath it to minimize line snags. At the seaward end is a refreshment stand. Cleaning facilities are a respectful distance away from that.

There is a fee parking lot on shore.

**Santa Monica** is the shore metropolis of the bay, and the site of both a state park beach and a commercial amusement park of scope and popularity.

Pacific Ocean Park is the amusement, a 28-acre playground, most of it built out over the water on piers. The theme is Neptune's Kingdom, and it has instructive moments among a raft of rides and exhibits that are mainly there for people to have fun with. The entry has live exhibits of sea animals (and some animated additions to the cast), and out on the pier are diving bells that go to the bottom of the bay. A single admission price covers all rides. The season is daily from mid-June to mid-September, and weekends in spring and fall while the weather holds.

Santa Monica Beach State Park flanks Pacific Ocean Park, and is the most popular of the bay beaches from the point of view of numbers. The park has picnic tables, fire rings, and playground equipment, and is handy to restaurants and all kinds of resort-type businesses.

**Will Rogers State Park** is beneath the Pacific Palisades (so close beneath them that slides once pushed the Coast Highway a few feet west, into some badly needed parking lots). Lifeguards and restrooms are on the beach, and restaurants line the highway nearby. It is the end of the populous shore, but not of the popular shore.

## THE OUTER REACHES

From the foot of Topanga Canyon Road west and north to Sequit Point on the Los Angeles-Ventura County Line, there lies a string of heavily used beaches that offers an added few places to swim, surf, fish, or sunbathe. The state beaches are small, with the exception of Leo Carillo State Park on the county line. With the same exception, all are day-use only.

**Las Tunas Beach State Park,** the first of these, is across the Coast Highway from the foot of Topanga Canyon Road. **Malibu Lagoon Beach State Park** adjoins Malibu, the last town on the way to the north county line. Both of these have lifeguard protection, and Malibu has the more protected waters of the two. On the point, clam diggers can scuffle hoe gravelly spots for rock cockles. **Surfrider Beach** two miles south, is named for the obvious reason.

**Point Dume Beach State Park,** a long, steep-sided finger of sandstone pointed uncertainly toward the south, is several miles past Malibu. It has flocks of pelicans and cormorants on rocks a few hundred yards offshore, and flocks of surfers hurtling toward broad, sandy beaches or paddling away from them. Swimming is good at this park, and so is tidepooling. The place is a bit lonely and bleak looking after all the urban backshore of the other beaches.

The other two parks adjoin State 1, the Coast Highway. This one is west of it, served by a hard-surface spur road.

**Leo Carrillo Beach State Park** straddles the highway, is the

# The artful dodge called surfing

To people who do not practice it, surfing is sheer lunacy. It requires spending long hours in chilly or plain cold sea water, struggling with a huge and heavy board of uncertain stability.

People who do practice the sport offer all kind of complex explanations concerning solitude, the complete test of strength and skill, and on like that. Pestered long enough, most of them admit that it comes down to one thing: Surfing is fun. The fun is spiced by knowing that only the skilled can do it, and by the constant potential danger, but fun it is.

If it is not easy to explain why people do it, it is at least possible to explain how they do.

The first requirement is the right kind of waves, which are called spilling breakers by oceanographers. This describes a wave that stays on the verge of breaking for a long time, but does not collapse into tumbling foam until it is within a few feet of the shore.

Spilling breakers result when clearly defined swells roll ashore over gently sloping underwater topography, and are usually made best by the presence of rocks or holes in the bottom, or by strong cross or counter currents.

Some of the water from the crest of these waves spills out on the face of the wave. This is the propulsion power of the surfer, who slides always downhill on the face of the wave, pushed along by the water spilling onto the back of the board at about the same speed as the advancing wave.

The surfer has it good when this occurs steadily. If he slows, the stern of the board gets into the fastest-moving water at the crest and is pushed forward to a center point on the wave's face. If he speeds ahead, the board enters slow water and drops back toward that center.

This is where skill enters the picture. The back end of the board tends to go faster than the front end, and it is the endless fight for balance that keeps a surfer up and riding toward the beach.

The greatest expression of skill, the sign of the virtuoso is "hanging ten." The ten which get hung are toes, over the nose of the board. It isn't a matter of going faster, but rather a matter of maintaining balance and direction from the least controllable part of the board.

San Diego beaches (Imperial, Sunset Cliffs, Pacific, Del Mar, Oceanside, San Onofre), and Santa Monica Bay beaches (Point Dume, Malibu, Redondo) are the centers of

*Coming in* on a wave and a prayer

the sport, where the waves demand high skill. Dozens of other beaches all along the California shore produce the three to five-foot waves that tax the capacities of novices and intermediates. North of Point Conception the water gets colder, but that seems to produce no effect on the hardy types who pursue this sport, except the occasional concession of wearing the top half of a wet suit. There are always a few board riders milling around Monterey Bay, Seal Rock in San Francisco, and even Crescent Beach at Crescent City.

The governing body of organized (competitor's clubs) surfing is the United States Surfing Association, P.O. Box 59, Redondo Beach, California.

The recommended textbook for newcomers, active and spectator, is *Surfing* by H. Arthur Klein (published by Lippincott).

first camping park north of Los Angeles, and is 12 miles from the nearest community, Malibu. Its spacious 1,500 acres kept it uncrowded for years after other Los Angeles beaches were doing land office business. But after the campsites were installed in 1960, new patrons flocked to it, and have kept coming back since.

The campsites are in foothills inland from the highway, the only drawback to the park since youngsters have to cross the high speed road to get down to the shore.

Once safely across the highway, the beach has beautiful

sandy sections for swimmers (it is only fitting that the park be named after a movie star-parks commissioner since it was itself a star of all kinds of South Seas movies in the innocent days of Old Hollywood when California was a stand-in for everywhere ).The beach also has outcrops of rock for fishermen, tidepoolers, and wave-watchers.

The diverse underwater topography also produces fair to good surfing.

Restrooms, dressing rooms, and a concession building mitigate the lack of a town nearby.

# Santa Barbara to Morro Bay

Point Conception is the magic dividing point for California's coast. South of it the climate is Mediterranean. North of it, matters grow progressively cooler.

Santa Barbara, the anchor point for most people who find themselves between Los Angeles and San Francisco, is most determinedly Mediterranean in its outlook.

This city, as much as San Diego, had Spanish beginnings. It treasures them even more. The annual civic celebration is designed to recall to local citizens that a measured slowness and a time to dance are important parts of daily living. Local leaders allow new industry only after it demonstrates that it will be neither smoky nor noisy. The population growth is controlled, too, by keeping new building at a certain level.

For all of that, it has navy missiles to port (Point Mugu) and air force missiles to starboard (Vandenberg AFB on Point Conception). The beaches between these rocket pads are for swimmers, surfers, picnickers, skin-divers, fishermen, and grunion hunters, except in a few places where oil rigs take over.

North of Point Conception a pair of adjoining bays have cooler water, and as one result have one of the world's tastiest clams, the Pismo. Pismo Beach and Morro Bay are mainly vacation centers for people who like to fish, or to dig clams. Swimmers, picnickers, and tidepoolers have much to occupy them in these bays, too.

## Santa Barbara

Santa Barbara is a town of such implausible charm that people who have yet to visit it do not always believe it exists. It does, in the midst of a stretch of seacoast much favored for its mildness by swimmers and much feared by mariners for its furies of wind and wave.

The implausible charm owes to the dedicated and to date successful efforts of the townspeople to retain and even improve upon Spanish beginnings. The seacoast is benign to swimmers and picnickers because both air and water temperatures are warm all summer, and because the adjacent countryside is full of innocent pleasures. It is malign to mariners because a dense fog habitually hangs offshore and because prevailing winds blow furiously through the funnel formed by the mainland on one side and the channel islands on the other. As a graveyard for ships, it ranks just a notch or two below the Columbia River Bar and the Golden Gate, a distinction achieved without a major port to help its reputation.

### THE NEARBY BEACHES

While Santa Barbara is no huge city, it still is an urban center of some size and its harbor and adjacent shore reflect that, especially looking eastward.

**Santa Barbara Harbor** between the breakwater and Stearns Wharf is not exactly virgin shore. Hundreds of small boats, both commercial fishermen and pleasure craft, tie up at the finger piers. The predictable amount of oil leakage and overside waste occurs, rendering the water less appetizing to swimmers. Still, the broad crescent of sand is a pleasant place to amble along with no pressing aim in mind.

The main allure for visitors is the sportfishing. Charter boats go out for relaxed days or half days of albacore and rock fishing in the lee of Santa Cruz Island.

**Leadbetter Beach** to windward of the breakwater is municipal and strongly swept by the surf. Its main use is by picnickers and sunbathers, but the hardy can swim or body surf handily enough. It can be reached from West Cabrillo Boulevard.

**Arroyo Burro** near the west city limits is a state beach operated by the county. Used by surf fishermen, swimmers, and picnickers, it is a sandy strip below a bluff that has some sheltering effect. Lifeguards patrol the 600-foot beach, and there are restrooms, barbecues, picnic tables and other facilities that make this a popular family beach.

**Goleta Beach State Park,** on a sandspit adjoining the campus of the University of California at Santa Barbara, is administered in the same way as Arroyo Burro and serves the same purpose except that shore fishing is little practiced and a sheltered cove is put to use by boaters. A charter boat for fishermen operates from this park.

The picnic ground is especially organized for large groups.

In the other direction from the harbor and Stearns Wharf are several more such beaches.

**East Beach** is at the end of the shore-paralleling segment of East Cabrillo Boulevard. With the exceptions of a few areas reserved for guests of specific motels or hotels, the whole sandy strip is publicly accessible from Stearns Wharf to the park area of East Beach.

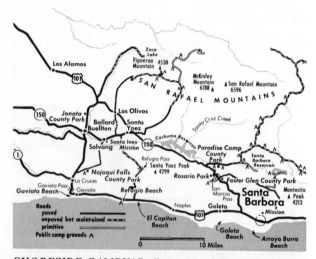

*SHORESIDE CAMPING: Emma Wood Beach State Park (200 units); El Capitan Beach State Park (85); Carpinteria Beach State Park (92 units, 25 trailer units). SHORESIDE ACCOMMODATIONS: Major concentrations on East Cabrillo Boulevard in Santa Barbara, and in Ventura. Others along highways. No lists available.*

*Broad crescent* of sand extends south from Santa Barbara small boat harbor

Behind the sand, tree-shaded picnic tables are scattered along a grassy strip between beach and road. Behind East Beach park area is the Andree Clark Bird Refuge. A children's zoo and playground rounds out the complex.

## EAST TO OXNARD

Each of the shore towns east of Santa Barbara has a beach park, beginning with Carpinteria and ending with Ventura.

**Carpinteria Beach State Park,** west off the freeway at the Carpinteria exit, is only 36 acres altogether, but one of the most-used parks in the region. It was, once, a bean field, but the State Division of Beaches and Parks wrought a new character with landscaping and sand. The park has a natural breakwater in the form of a reef a couple of thousand yards offshore, which makes it a safe beach for children to swim. The same reef harbors spiny lobsters and abalones, thus attracting skin divers, and on the shore a fishing pier offers still another diversion. The grunion run at this beach is one of the best in southern California.

The campsites and picnic areas are set in a grove of trees just behind the long, sand arc of the shore.

**Emma Wood Beach State Park** is half the size of Carpinteria, and rather less pleasantly developed, Still, the swimming is good, and it does have plenty of campsites. The highway runs along the edge of the park, which is two miles north of Ventura.

**San Buenaventura Beach** in the city of Ventura is odd among these beaches in that it is a pebble rather than a sandy shore. Otherwise, it is much like its mates north and south. A mile long, shaded from behind by trees, it has lifeguards, concessions, shore fishing, fire rings, picnic tables, and a play area for children. Shore fishing is reasonably good, and a nearby pier is home port for deep sea party boats.

The navy takes up much of the shore south of Ventura with Port Hueneme and Point Mugu. (The navy's growing interest in that greater ocean of space has centered here, causing rapid growth in the towns of Ventura and Oxnard and a great sense of identity with missilery, everywhere evident in the names of local business.) Port Hueneme has a public harbor, and there is a new state beach, McGrath, four miles south of Ventura.

## WEST TO POINT CONCEPTION

There are no towns along the shore between Goleta and Gaviota. Beyond Gaviota the U. S. Air Force controls the shore and huge acreages behind it all the way around Point Conception, in the interests of flinging rockets safely and secretly aloft. The water stays warm at the several park areas along this shore, and the patronage is ample.

**El Capitan Beach State Park** is the first of three parks north of Goleta. It is only a few miles north of that university community, and its towering row of sycamores alongside the highway is a landmark to people who pass this way with any frequency. The park has 10,000 feet of ocean frontage, most of it sandy and safe for swimming, some of it rocky tidepools and outcrops that give the surf something to get worked up about.

The park has lifeguard service, fire pits, picnic tables, and restrooms in addition to its campsites. The only drawback is poison oak along some of the walking paths between campground and beach.

**Refugio Beach State Park,** 20 miles north of Santa Barbara and two miles north of El Capitan, is administered by the county. It is a camping park with points of interest for swimmers and surf fishermen. The park facilities include lifeguards, barbecue pits, picnic tables, restrooms, and several games courts.

**Gaviota Beach State Park** is yet another 10 miles west of Santa Barbara, and has facilities for swimmers, skin divers, boaters, and fishermen. Only eight acres, with 500 feet of beach front, the park adjoins a pier from which a charter boat operates for day-long fishing excursions among the Channel Islands. There is also a small boat hoist.

The picnic facilities surround a central pergola. The campsites are without hookups.

A concession supplements local restaurants and shops.

# Pismo Beach and surrounds

This is the home of the Pismo clam. The broad, surf-swept arc of the bay provides an ideal environment from the point of view of the clams. Their only trouble is that the shore is so accessible to clam-loving human types.

One result is that the greater part of the beds are now a preserve. Only the north end of the state park, north of Oceano, is open to digging. But that is still the main reason visitors come to these pleasant towns, with their wide and level beaches.

**Pismo Beach State Park** has some six miles of shore running south from the town of Pismo Beach, through Oceano, and on into the north end of California's best and largest expanse of sand dunes. The camping area is sometimes partly overrun by sand, in fact, to the eternal amusement of children who like to run around in it. It is the dunes that makes the park a noteworthy one in the absence of clams. Its other recreational pursuits include

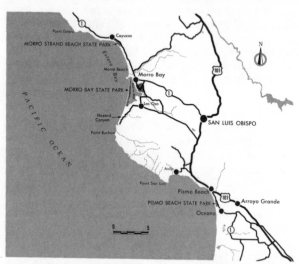

**SHORESIDE CAMPING:** *Pismo Beach State Park (143 units, 89 trailer units); Morro Bay State Park (115 units, 20 trailer units); San Simeon (25 units on the shore below the Hearst Castle).* **SHORESIDE ACCOMMODATIONS:** *Pismo Beach-Oceano, Morro Bay, Cayucos, Cambria, San Simeon. No lists available.*

*Digging clams requires varied skills*

One good thing about clams is steaming them in a bucket over a beach fire and eating them right there, after they have been dipped in butter. Another good thing is canning ground clam meat for thick, steaming winter-night chowders. But one of the best things about clams is digging them.

Clam digging is a vigorous but safe exercise for a loner, a picnic crowd, or a family of all ages. There are enough different kinds of clams on enough different kinds of beaches to guarantee some digging to anybody who can get to a representative strip of salt water beach.

The equipment consists in a gunny sack or other carrying device, sneakers, a fishing license (in California), and a rake, hoe, shovel, or pick while the digging is going on, and a change of clothes and something warming to drink after it is done.

There are four general techniques to accommodate four general conditions. On sandy beaches, diggers tap with shovel handles, the vibration of which causes clams to withdraw their siphons, leaving a bubble, or "show." Digging is always to the seaward side of a show.

In mud flats, the siphon show is plainer, and sometimes is a fairly sizable depression in the sand. In the soggy working conditions, many diggers like to use a five-gallon can with both ends cut out to shore up the sides of the excavation.

On gravel bars and reefs, rake through gravel deposits in the rock with a triangular shaped hoe.

All digging is best done on minus tides, from one hour before low tide to one hour after. It is possible to dig on any low tide, but easily reached beds are usually kept thinly populated by frequent digging. Most clams are governed by seasons in California, and each of the coast states has daily bag and possession limits. These vary enough that local inquiry is the only safe way. Old hands along this coast are well aware of the summer menace of red tides. The red tide is a very complex

# Pismo or bent-nose... a clam is for digging

*Pismos are raked from shallow water, forked up from surf. Gapers go deep in sand. Smaller clams lie beneath surface*

change in the balance of micro-organisms in sea water, and for clammers its important effect is to poison the flesh of clams living in ocean waters. Red tides have less effect on bay clams. At any event, many beaches are quarantined during summer months when red tides are likely, and newcomers to any along California should check into the matter before digging and eating clams.

The following is a roster of commonly dug clams.

Bent-nosed clam, averaging two inches across shell, is tough and can often be found where other varieties cannot endure. It inhabits muddy bays the length of the coast at depths from six to eight inches. The meat has a good flavor, particularly in a chowder. It takes two days' holding in salt water for the clam to flush mud from its stomach.

Gaper clam, known as horse clam in the Northwest, weighs as much as three pounds. It is found in firm, clean bay sand the length of the coast, and can burrow to a depth of two feet in that environment. It squirts a mighty jet of water when disturbed. Its flavorful meat is covered by tough skin, which can be peeled off after a few seconds of boiling the clam. The hefty neck is best used ground for chowder. The shells make dandy ash trays.

Geoduck, pronounced gooey-duck, is the largest clam in sight. Heavyweights scale out at 10 pounds. It lives in muddy bay bottoms (mostly on sand bars), in the Northwest more commonly than California. The digger's hole goes very deep, and usually has to be supported by a metal sleeve. The clam has a skin much like the gaper's, and should be used similarly.

Heart cockle (the clam with the rib-knit shell) averages two inches in width, and possesses a highly individual flavor. Some people like it, some do not. The clam is an easy one to find at or near the surface of rock-dotted sand in bay tideflats or protected outer coast.

Jackknife clams resemble razor clams, but are smaller. They are found from a foot to 16 inches deep in quiet

bays from Santa Barbara south. The clam is often used as bait by commercial fishermen.

Pismo clams are the ecological counterpart to the razor clam of the Northwest, but they look nothing like the razor. The shells are very heavy and circular. The weight of an adult is about a pound and a half. The clam exists only on surf-swept sand beaches from Monterey Bay to Pismo Bay. Most beds are seriously depleted, and some are closed to digging. The clams live about six inches beneath the sand surface, and are best gotten with a special rake. The meat has a distinctive, sweet flavor. It goes well fried, in fritters, or in chowders.

The razor clam is explored in some detail on page 96.

Rock Cockle, ranging up to two inches, lives in bay bottoms all along the coast, often near bay mouths. Many times it concentrates in gravelly areas. This is the steamed clam of northwest restaurants, and that is the way it tastes best. The local name for it in the Northwest is littleneck.

Rough Piddock, a rock-boring clam also known as the rock oyster in Oregon, burrows in stiff clay or soft rock, from whence it is quarried with hammer and chisel. It does not occur in any predictable pattern, but shows up in many rip-rap breakwaters in Oregon. It goes reasonably well in a stew, where its stout flavor can be subdued by other ingredients.

Softshell clam (or mud clam) burrows in muddy bay water north of Monterey. It will almost always be found where a tideflat is malodorous, and it has to be dug with careful horizontal swipes with a shovel blade to avoid breaking its fragile shell. It should be cleaned and skinned, and put in a stew if it is to be enjoyed.

Washington clam, also called the Martha Washington, grows to five inches width in mud flats all along the coast (gravelly or otherwise). It usually stays at a depth of eight inches. This clam is good steamed.

*Hungry pelican makes a pre-historic plunge into Pismo Bay after a fleeing fish. Score one*

surf fishing and muskrat watching (the latter in a marshy lagoon). Swimming is safe but chilly in summer.

At the north end of the park, in the town of Pismo Beach, there is a pier. Fish can be caught from it, and so can party boats for deep sea fishing excursions.

South of the park, there is little access to the shore until State 1 rejoins the shore south of Point Conception. One exception is Point Sal, an undeveloped state beach west of Santa Maria. The other is the wee town of Surf, a boat harbor surrounded by Vandenberg Air Force Base.

**Avila** nestles within the north arc of San Luis Obispo Bay, a small town with a majority of peace-seeking retired couples in its population. A state-owned, county-operated park on the beach front is small, but organized for the active. For one thing, a freak chance provides very warm water along the shore in this cove. Its temperature is always above 60° and frequently gets into the low 70° range, an ideal state of affairs for people who like to swim in oceans but find the Pacific too brisk for most of its shore length.

Other facilities include a fishing pier, picnic tables, fire rings, charter boats, a launching ramp, a rental concession for surf boards, crab nets, and other such salty gear.

As if those merits were not enough, the town is set in some hills of surpassing scenic worth, and the drive to it is a pleasure in itself. It is two miles west from U.S. 101 on a sign-posted county road.

# Morro Bay

Once it was just a waypoint for people who liked to drive the long, slow way between San Francisco and Los Angeles, but Morro Bay's charms proved memorable enough to pull former passers-through back for longer looks. Now it does a brisk annual business with vacationers who would have no substitute.

Its charms are several. Morro Bay is one of the few remaining places where it is permitted to dig Pismo Clams (and one of the few remaining places with any to dig). The long sandy spit pointing straight at Morro Rock forms a good natural harbor for small boats and fishing vessels at the same time it offers vastly different kind of shore than the rocky stuff south at Hazard Canyon or across at Morro Rock. The state park golf course gives respite from shore patrolling. San Simeon is only a few miles north. Pismo Beach is even less distant to the south.

## TOWN, ROCK, AND BAY

The town of Morro Bay sits at the head of the bay that carries its name, just across from Morro Rock. The geography is a bit confusing. Morro Bay is the little bay inside the sand spit. The big crescent bay outside is called Estero Bay.

The town is headquarters for a commercial fishing fleet. In the municipal harbor are party boats and rental boats for sport fishermen, as well as a fee launching facility.

**Morro Bay State Park** rather completely surrounds the town. The rock is one part of it. The sand spit is another, and the inshore side of the bay south of town is yet a third element.

The rock connects to the mainland by causeway, and it is the outer side of the causeway that provides some of the area's best clam digging on minus tides. There is a broad, sandy beach running north from the rock that harbors the Pismo in something like abundant numbers.

An enormous power plant with corrugated metal buildings and towering smokestacks detracts just a little from the scenic qualities of Morro Rock, once called the Gibraltar of California. Some of the rocky coves along the causeway leading out to this structure provide as good shorefishing as the area offers (perch and flounder mainly, with lesser numbers of cabezone, jack smelt, and ling cod). Locally wise fishermen do not venture out onto the harbor jetty to fish. The wave action is unpredictable out there.

The sandy spit is about 500 yards across, and dunes where the tide can't reach. The spit is all park, but its south end is a clam preserve. A road runs around the bottom of the bay, but that is an ordinary way to get there. A less routine mode is the clam taxi, which shuttles between the marina at the foot of Fourth Street and a marker post

*Morro Rock is a backdrop to fishing vessels*

*Protected fishing inside Morro Bay breakwater*

on the spit. It operates the year around whenever the weather permits, hauling clammers, shore fishermen, and drift hunters for a dollar a head (plus 50 cents for a clam rake if need be). It departs to catch the ebbing tide, and returns on a pre-arranged time, or when the party re-assembles at a marker post.

Picnic tables near the landing area are a pleasant grace note to the whole enterprise.

The largest part of the park acreage is on the east shore of the bay a mile south of town. In this section are the camping areas, the golf course ("Poor Man's Pebble" as it is sometimes known), and picnic sites. The major part of the park is atop a bluff, from whence the views are dandy ones.

The southern end of the bay is the best place to look for shorebirds and sea birds. Loons, grebes, gulls, and cormorants predominate.

**Hazard Canyon** is not a park. Rather, it is a pleasantly isolated stretch of rocky shore three and a half miles south of the village of Los Osos. The most westerly road available is the one to take. It is paved and easy to drive. A wide dirt shoulder marks the head of the quarter-mile trail down the eucalyptus-lined canyon. The rock outcrops shelve gently into the sea, forming a few tidepools big enough to accommodate rubber rafts, and a great many smaller ones. The beach is open enough to walk a good distance in either direction at low tide, and it has periodic sandy pockets sheltered from the winds that normally blow in these parts.

## NORTH OF MORRO BAY

For some 30 miles north, the coast continues to be hospitable to visitors in one fashion or another. There are several more beach towns, parks, and points of interest before the topography gets precipitous after San Simeon.

**Morro Beach** and **Paso Robles Beach** lie north of the main resort area, but extend it to a degree. The publicly accessible shore in these areas is a mixture of rocky outcrops and sandy pockets. The clam population begins to thin out a bit as Point Estero begins to exert a calming influence on the surf.

**Morro Strand Beach State Park** upholds the general trend of the shore toward a mixture of rocks and sand. It is nowhere near so highly developed as Morro Bay State Park to the south, but it combines with the resort facilities at Cayucos just next door to make a reasonably complete place to spend a day or more. The main park activities are surf fishing and swimming or skin diving.

**Atascadero Beach State Park,** nearby, is similar in character to Morro Strand.

**Cayucos Beach,** locally operated and just to the north of the park, has dressing rooms, a playground for children, and other civil improvements. A party boat operates from the town harbor for sport fishermen.

The shore is mainly for swimmers. Skin diving is only fair, and the beach between Big Cayucos Creek and Old Creek is yet another Pismo clam preserve.

The town itself, larger than its lonely location would seem to indicate, is set pleasantly within a ring of the low, rolling, and sparsely treed hills that typify this whole region. In addition to the usual run of resort services, the city has a municipal fishing pier.

**Cambria,** 14 miles upcoast and faced out to sea, is set in a small cove rimmed all about by tall, steep bluffs. There are more trees at this point along the coast than there are farther south, and fewer buildings. Cambria used to be a last stop before the state acquired San Simeon as a park and permitted some commercial buildings in that neighborhood, and it still draws a fair share of people on a leisurely trip up or down State Highway 1. Abalone hunters find the picking good.

A county park has picnic facilities and a heated swimming pool, both right on the beach.

**San Simeon Creek Beach State Park** is slightly more than two miles north of Cambria, and almost six miles south of William Randolph Hearst's castle. The park is a long sand beach at the foot of bluffs (the top of the bluffs is the beach of pre-history). The park proper is between Leffingwell Creek and San Simeon Creek, where there are picnic facilities and restrooms, but the road north and south of those limits has pullouts from which vigorous explorers can clamber down to hunt for drift, rocks, or the occasional tidepool.

This is a fine, foggy, cold, wet, and windy place where an inlander can get a proper exposure to this moody ocean in its most habitual temper.

*San Simeon* castle is way up on the hills above the sea, a fitting manor for that great baron of American journalism, William Randolph Hearst. The Old Man, as he was known to his innumerable staffers, is gone both as an individual and a type, but his showplace remains. It is worth seeing, and it is being seen. In fact, the only sure way to see it is to write well in advance for reservations, to: Public Tours Reservation Office, P.O. Box 2390, Sacramento 95811. The current fee for tour and reservation is $3.

The castle itself is the reason for being in the neighborhood, but since it is forbidden to take picnic lunches or other food into its grounds, the presence of a beach park below it is indeed handy.

North of here, Piedras Blancas light is a place to contemplate the sea. It is open weekends, 1-4 p.m. After Piedras Blancas, it is Big Sur Or Bust.

## Getting the picnic there

*Travois* can be dragged to site, then set up as wind barrier. Pole is good in rough places

At a great many state and county parks the formal picnic facilities are fine to behold, and comfortable, too. But it isn't really a beach picnic without a good deal of staggering about to find a wind-sheltered log remote from the crowd (preferably on a hidden sandy beach).

When the beach picnic is a simple affair, wieners and sandy buns and something to wash them down, it is just a question of carting a small box.

But when the picnic is a gilt-edged, four-course, fit-for-a-king thing, the problems of transport want good solutions. Here are a few.

The picnic on a pole will draw at least one snicker from an onlooker (May he choke on a stale wiener bun), but it is an unusually orderly way to transport a complex meal of hot and cold dishes. All that is required is a stout pole (bamboo cannot be beaten, but any stout 1-inch diameter pole will do) of six, eight, or ten feet, and enough thermos jugs, baskets, and hampers to hold all the food and trimmings. The catch is that all the containers need curved handles so they will suspend properly.

The travois is more elaborate, but more versatile. It is an adaptation of an Indian device, pronounced "travvy" no matter what l'Academie Francaise has to say, that can be dragged very easily along a sandy beach or a gravelly one. In rough spots, two people can carry it, stretcher style. Any type of container at all can be dumped into it. If the original lashup is made so the side poles can be removed easily, the travois can be converted quickly into a wind shelter once at the picnic spot.

A camp cot does very well as a carrier on rough terrain, and can be used as a low table to keep food out of the sand when the meal is served.

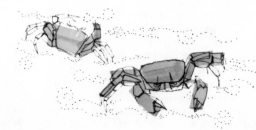

# Monterey, ageless charms

Most residents of the civilized world know something about Monterey. Any port with two centuries of contact with explorers, missionaries, seafarers, Yankee businessmen, and professional golfers has to have widely advertised charms. Monterey has them, in town or somewhere near.

The area lives up to its reputation so convincingly that it is or has been home to such improbably diverse talents as Henry Miller, Robinson Jeffers, Kim Novak, Hank Ketcham, and Gus Arriola among a population of 80,000. It is a vacation goal of some three million visitors annually.

The hotels are filled on one summer weekend after another, but an odd thing is that the shore seldom gets desperately crowded in any season. This in spite of the fact that Carmel and Big Sur have some of the world's most beautiful seascapes.

One reason is the amount and quality of inshore diversion: The Crosby golf tournament in January, the Laguna Seca Road Races in late April or early May, the Carmel Bach Festival in July, and the Monterey Jazz Festival in September, to say nothing of the excellent shops and restaurants all year around. The special events weekends are nearly hopeless without advance reservations.

Another reason for relatively sparse use of the shore is the weather and water. The water temperature hovers near 55°, creeping up toward 58° in August and sinking toward 52° in February. The summer air temperatures are only slightly higher, mainly because of the celebrated fog bank which rolls ashore almost daily from late May until sometime in September. The fall months often have temperatures in the high 70's, but even the brisk days are sparkling clear a good part of the time. Winter temperatures hover in the mid 40's to mid 50's,

## The Three Towns

Packed into a relatively small area, the three towns of Monterey, Pacific Grove, and Carmel have a balanced mixture of sandy and rocky beaches. Counting Del Monte forest, they also have a pleasant mixture of harbor, residential and undeveloped shore.

### PENINSULA BEACH AREAS

Beginning with Monterey and proceeding along the coast, these are publicly accessible beaches south to Asilomar.

**Monterey Municipal Beach,** east of the Municipal Wharf is part of a broad, gently sloping sandy crescent that stretches almost a mile. A municipal lifeguard (summers) watches over the first few hundred yards. Beyond that, increasingly stiff longshore currents and mounting surf make swimming inadvisable. However, strollers, sunbathers, and picnickers can go as far as a small point just past a cluster of fuel storage tanks visible from the wharf.

The beach next to the wharf is especially good for families with small children. In addition to having good conditions for wading (in sun-warmed shallow water) and the activity of the boats, a spacious municipal parking lot is adjacent, and Dennis the Menace Playground is but a short stroll across Del Monte Avenue, one block up Camino el Estero, and north across the bridge.

Open beach fires are prohibited, but hibachis and camp stoves can be used by picnickers who want their food hot.

Out near the fuel tanks, the surf gets active enough to draw a number of reasonably adept board riders.

**Fisherman's Wharf** and **Municipal Wharf,** side by side, are not exactly beaches, but they are worth a beach explorer's time, especially if he has children who like a bit of action in their diets.

A few raffish personalities from the local sea lion herds beg handouts at the offshore end of Fisherman's Wharf, where 25-cent bags of fish are sold to abet such vagrancy. This is as close as anybody can get to free and untamed specimens of the animal, if not noble ones. They advertise their presence with baying that resonates for blocks around.

Each morning shortly after dawn party boats laden with sport fishermen put out, to return in early afternoon after a day of mixed salmon and bottom fishing, with the accent on the latter. Their ticket offices are on Fisherman's Wharf, which also supports fish stalls, restaurants, and curio shops in numbers.

Municipal Wharf strikes a more sober note. Seven canneries on it take anchovy, cod, kingfish, herring, salmon, sole, and tuna from the holds of the commercial fleet.

*SHORESIDE CAMPING: Only in Pacific Valley Forest Camp (15 units) 62 miles south of Monterey. Pfeiffer-Big Sur State Park (218 units) has no ocean front, but is accessible to the shore. SHORESIDE ACCOMMODATIONS: Pacific Grove, Carmel, Big Sur. More inshore at Monterey, Carmel. Write Monterey Peninsula C of C, P.O. Box 489, Monterey, for lists or reservations.*

*Sea lion wins* contest for lunch at Monterey Wharf

Even fishermen are sometimes awed by the rare creatures that turn up in their nets. On occasion they will haul a few of these inedible rarities back to port and put them out on the pier in view of passers-by, whose normal reaction is to circle the spot gingerly. The land-bound human tends to think of life as a basically mammalian process, and is little comforted to view such unlovely things wriggle.

Dropline fishing from this pier often produces plentiful catches of sunfish, jack smelt, and tom cod, and is much practiced by the youth of the neighborhood.

West of the piers, the shore is either industrial or privately held, as far as the beach at Lover's Point in Pacific Grove. (From the east city limits of Pacific Grove to its municipal beach, the rocky shore is the preserve of Hopkins Marine Station of Stanford University.)

**Pacific Grove Municipal Beach** is a small, sheltered cove in the lee of Lover's Point. The beach is sandy and safe for swimming, but the water is so cold that even hardy natives often prefer the heated water of the pool just above the beach. The beach belongs to lizard-brown sunbathers.

At one side of the beach, a concrete pier serves as operations base of a fleet of glass-bottomed boats that takes visitors out on tours of offshore marine gardens. The water of this bay is uncommonly clear, and it supports an uncommonly diverse and numerous marine life. These boats, for a modest fee, offer the best look a man can get short of diving. Trips are only on the calm days of summer. Winter crowds are too slim, especially when storm waves break over the pier.

Surfers congregate to ride three to five foot waves from a spot just inside the tip of Lover's Point to the end of the pier, a distance of about 200 yards. Skilled practitioners of the chilly art ride the waves until it appears inevitable they will end up superimposed on the end wall of the pier. But, no, calamity's clutch fails and the rubber-suited hero paddles out for another attempt. From a dry perch on the rocky point, it is a grand diversion, with the action close below the rocks.

From the outer tip of the point, rock fishermen do fair business with the usual run of rock fishes.

**Lover's Point to Point Pinos,** a stretch of nearly two miles, has no formal park facilities, but all of it offers unlimited access and bountiful enjoyment to beach hikers, tidepool explorers, and rock fishermen. At the Lover's Point end, rocks plunge steeply to the water from the road level of Ocean View Boulevard, a drop of 10 to 15 feet. Heading west, the beach becomes progressively flatter and sandier, and the main force of the waves spends itself on offshore rocks and shoals that also form some fine tide-pools. At one time the seaward edge of Pacific Grove seemed to be disappearing at an alarming rate, while the inter-tidal population of animals suffered serious depletion. The city found itself forced to prohibit all collecting, but especially of large rocks and marine invertebrates.

Although Ocean View Boulevard parallels the shore from Lover's Point to the edge of the lighthouse reservation, the city had the happy thought to provide a walking path and intermittent benches all along the shore, between the street and the sea. At low tide, the distance can be covered at water's edge with some scrambling around or over rocks.

**Point Pinos Light** stands at the westward extreme of all

*Swim, sunbathe, boat, or surf at Lover's Point*

this, in the middle of a golf course that offers all kinds of sand wedge practice to the errant. In an era when lighthouses are being decommissioned and left as scenic vestiges, this one still burns and welcomes visitors from 1 to 4 p.m. on weekends. It can be reached by going west to the end of Lighthouse Avenue (the main street of Pacific Grove), or from the shoreside roads.

**Asilomar Beach State Park** is an extension of the Hotel and Conference Grounds, and is much used by relaxing conferees, but is capacious enough to hold a great many additional visitors to its shore. The beach runs almost true north and south between Point Pinos and Del Monte Forest. The north end (a short row of shoreside homes disconnects it from other Pacific Grove beach areas) has a long, nearly flat shelf of rock that extends well offshore. Great amounts of this rock become exposed on extreme minus tides, to the delight of tidepool explorers. This is, in fact, the "Great Tidepool" where Doc gathered many animals as described in *Cannery Row.* The southern part of the beach is a wide sandy crescent backed by dunes. It attracts a great many surf fishermen.

The collecting of marine animals from this beach is as rigidly forbidden as it is elsewhere around the peninsula. However it is not forbidden to scramble about the rocks. Sometimes the surf will keep a man from wanting to get out there, but on an ebbing tide on a calm day, this is a great place to go out and get soaked in the interests of peering at sea anemones, or brushing giant red sea urchins with a blunt, soft piece of wood to stimulate a defense against a starfish. (Starfish are the mortal enemies of sea urchins, which seldom win a contest between the two, but which put up a spirited defense with hundreds of stinging jaws called pedicellariae. They flatten their sharp spines away from the point of attack to use them. Each jaw can bite only once, so experiments along these lines should be designed to leave the animal some defenses while it regenerates these specialized cells.)

*Point Pinos Light is a beacon to boats and tourists*

## SEVENTEEN MILE DRIVE

Between Pacific Grove and Carmel, a shoreline distance of 10 miles, is the huge private development called Del Monte Properties, or Del Monte Forest. The corporate ownership has constructed a considerable length of shoreside road (the greater part of the famous drive), a wholly appropriate building called the Camera Obscura, several difficult to gruelling golf courses, and nothing that interferes with one of the world's fine seascapes (forgiving the tree-screened presence of a sand plant on the Pacific Grove boundary).

Visiting auto tourists can, for a modest fee, drive into the area, picnic (no fires) on the shore at any of the designated areas; observe the offshore antics of sea birds, sea lions, and seals; ramble along on some fine rocky beaches in quest of shells; puzzle over the Monterey cypress and its rare growth habits, and, for sheer diversion, study an unusual and unwilling form of shore life, the wayward golfer.

**The Camera Obscura** (Latin: darkened room) is a good place to start. It is a round coolie hat of a building with one door, no windows, and a sloping roof with high peak and broad overhang. This walk-in camera employs the same principle as the photographic camera, but records its

*Horseback riding allowed in winter at Carmel Beach*

impressions on a circular screen on the floor rather than celluloid film. The images move and shift as the lens rotates (while a recorded voice offers commentary).

The camera operates continuously from 8 a.m. until dark each day, and there is no admission charge to the structure designed by architect John Carl Warnecke.

What the lens views includes Bird Rock, the more distant Seal Rock, and Fanshell Beach away to the south, as well as parts of Cypress Point Club and the Shore Course of the Monterey Peninsula Country Club. The building adjoins a picnic area.

On Bird Rock dwell considerable numbers of Brandt's cormorant (the same bird that is a professional fisherman for the Japanese), several smaller cormorants, a variety of gulls, and fortunately flightless sea lions.

Seal Rock harbors both sea lions and the small harbor seal, also called the leopard seal.

**Fanshell Beach** gets its name from the abundant presence of these shells after winter storms—and doubtless causes summer visitors to wonder if the shore looks like a fanshell because by the time they arrive it is picked clean.

Several other areas are set aside for the enjoyment by all comers of the superb seascapes. Most of the views take full advantage of particularly wind-battered examples of the famous Monterey cypress trees.

**Point Joe,** where Seventeen-Mile Drive begins to head inland at the north end of the shore area, has its own, historically grisly charm. The appearance of the point from the sea resembles the entrance to Monterey Bay so closely that pre-radar navigators could and often did make the mistake on fog-shrouded approaches. The bones of the vessels thus lost are disappeared.

Near the same point, unusual underwater formations cause surface currents and waves to boil and bubble all out of proportion to prevailing conditions. This turbulent patch of water called "The Restless Sea" is plainly visible from the shore.

## CARMEL'S SANDY BEACHES

Carmel for years was an English seaside retreat, a charming thatch of cottages on a green hill above the sea. In winter it is still something like that, but in summer it is more like Brighton in the matter of crowds.

**Carmel Beach** most of it to the south of the main street of the village, is a broad and sandy crescent that attracts great numbers of sunbathers and picnickers when the weather is kindly, and great numbers of beach walkers no matter what the weather is doing. In winter, the city permits horses to be ridden along the strand (October to April).

## How to see a sea otter

Any clear day of autumn can be a good day for spotting sea otters along the central coast of California. It takes considerable patience, and a good pair of field glasses or binoculars.

The sea otter is a shy and wary creature that spends its day floating in the offshore kelp beds, its shiny bobbing head almost indistinguishable from shiny bobbing kelp floats. When the otters do reveal themselves, they are antic characters whose eating and play habits are endearingly human. Practical jokes have a role in sea otter society. One will dunk a neighbor and steal his food. Another pair will play something much akin to leapfrog. Sometimes a lone animal will do nip-ups for the sheer pleasure of it.

When a sea otter eats, he separates himself from the herd (which may number from three to a hundred or more) and forages on his own. He dives gracefully to the bottom, selects a sea urchin, abalone, chiton, clam, or crab, and brings it to the surface to eat.

One of the few animals known to use a tool consistently, the sea otter employs a rock to prepare his food. He places the rock on his chest and cracks the shellfish against it with a sweep of the forepaw, or vice versa. Once the shell is cracked, he picks out the desired meat.

When a sea otter senses danger (from large sharks, principally) he seeks shelter in the kelp. When he sleeps, he shrewdly protects himself by wrapping strands of firmly anchored kelp about his body to prevent being washed ashore.

This animal bears little resemblance to seals or sea lions, and is not related to them. Rather he is kin to the river otter, weasel, skunk, badger, mink, marten, and ermine. His Latin name is *Enhydra lutris*, and he grows to four and-a-half feet long, with a maximum weight of 80 pounds (females reach about 45 pounds). A newborn

pup is 20 inches long and weighs three to five pounds. The face is conspicuously flat, and usually lighter in color than the body. Ears are rounded. The tail is about a foot long. His paddlelike hind feet are webbed. The fur of the adult is a rich, lustrous brown and it is that characteristic that nearly caused his extermination by Russian fur traders in the mid-nineteenth century. He yowls like a cat.

Because he is so rare, the animal is protected by law within the 90 miles of coastal water that is his regular range. The herd numbers about 400 animals at present, as against about 90 when it was rediscovered off Monterey in 1938 (the otter having been thought extinct for years previous). The fine for molesting, injuring, or killing a sea otter is $1,000 and a year in prison.

The premier watching station is Point Lobos Reserve, south of Carmel, but many bluffs along State 1 do almost as well. In Point Lobos, the best spots are the shore on the south side of the point and around Gibson Cove. On the highway, favored spots are the bluffs near Yankee Point; Malpaso Creek; Granite Creek (park near the north end of the bridge); Garrapata Creek; above the mouth of Palo Colorado Canyon; Bixby Creek; Hurricane Point; Parkington Point; Anderson Creek; Burns Creek; Hot Springs Creek (near John Little State Park); Gamboa Point; Point Gorda, and Salmon Creek.

U.S. Geological Survey quadrangle maps, all in the 15-minute series, are Monterey, Point Sur, Lucia, and Cape San Martin. They show all points named.

Some veteran watchers consider the hours from dawn to 9 a.m. and from late afternoon until sunset the best times, but the animals are around all day, in the calm of the kelp beds or sometimes in the seething water around rocks. A concentration of gulls sometimes hovers over feeding otters, to catch crumbs.

*Point Lobos Reserve, a scenic spot for picnics—a spectacular setting for hiking, picture-taking*

Not many are hardy enough to attempt swimming in these chilly waters, and rip currents ("undertows" in the less sophisticated times when local warning signs were painted) can be too tough for any but the most experienced salt water swimmers. These currents are weakest on an incoming tide.

The Carmel beach seems to end at the rocky point upon which a dramatic house faces out to sea. It doesn't. There is another section of beach south of that point, and it is of some interest to students of oceanography for the fact that is has a very steep face caused by violent winter surf. This steep face remains all summer, as many as eight feet high, when gentler waves produce a narrow shelf below. The height of the face is an accurate measure of the height of winter waves that form it.

**Carmel River Beach State Park** curls inside a loop of State Highway 1 where the road drops to sea level about a mile south of Carmel. Sandy, battered by strong surf, and without facilities, it is in the main a haunt of surf fishermen. The lagoon formed by the debouching Carmel River allows children to splash and wade in tolerably warm water when the sun beats back the summer fog bank. Picnickers can have open beach fires.

# South to Big Sur

Just south of Carmel, the rolling hills that rim Monterey Bay give way to Santa Lucia Mountains, the steep sides of which press tight against the shore all the way to Morro Bay. The northerly quarter of this coast is known as the Big Sur Country, one of the most splendidly bleak places in the United States.

## POINT LOBOS RESERVE STATE PARK

The park, five miles south of Monterey on State 1, looks very little like the tamed shoreline of Monterey Peninsula proper, and yet is not as foreboding as the coast on south.

Its many-fingered headland is steep and rocky, and it used to stick out a long way farther until the waves cut through a soft spot, and left some offshore islands for the use of sea lions and shorebirds.

The rocks that make it up are curiously diverse—sandstone here, recemented conglomerate there, granite somewhere else, and much of the sedimentary strata turned up at sharp and sometimes contradictory angles. Spray-scoured sections fringe on the lunar.

Seawater churns briskly through gaps and over low spots, becoming so highly aerated that it can and does support unusually dense clusters of intertidal and shallow water life forms.

In contrast to the white water outside the tip, there are several still coves of deep water. One of these was a headquarters for nineteenth century whalers, and they left behind as tangible evidence a shack that is now grayed and weathered into a water colorists' cliche. Panhandling squirrels live next to the parking lot near the shack in Carmelo Cove, round bellies ample evidence of their abilities along this line.

Offshore, to the south of the longest headland, huge kelp beds serve as home to a considerable number of sea otters, and everywhere on the park shore, but especially at Pelican Point on its south boundary, brown pelicans, Brandt's cormorants, and gulls abound.

Most of the sea lions live on the rocks off the point named Lobos (a longer one called Pinnacle lies just north),

*Big Sur fog is seldom on vacation when tourists are*          *Barking sea lions like to camp on Big Sur coast*

and scrambling about on the craggy rocks of the point is one of the park's finest rewards for the physically vigorous tidepool explorer.

One of the primary reasons this site was selected as a park preserve is the fine stand of Monterey cypress fringing the outer reaches of the headland. These trees, which some scientists think are the last few natural survivors of a line that is on the verge of extinction, buttress their main limbs to counter sea winds. It is a rare if not unique response to environment among trees, and the resultant appearance is unusually photogenic for people who like stark, linear compositions. Another tree making a similar stand against extinction is the Torrey pine, similarly preserved in Torrey Pines State Park north of San Diego.

Picnic tables are grouped in several areas throughout the park, both in exposed and sheltered locations, but no fires are permitted. Rock fishermen can try their luck along the shores of Carmelo Cove, or other beaches by permission. Divers can explore after gaining permission at park headquarters, but all plant and animal life in the park is protected, and nothing may be injured or taken.

Walking trails criss-cross the park in all directions, and visitors are requested to stay on them to preserve some of the delicate plant communities.

## THE BIG SUR COUNTRY

It is more for people who like to look at the ocean than it is for people who like to do something about it. There is a widely-known colony of painters, writers, and would-be's with roots going well back in the history of this place that will likely be one of the last in the state to become populous. But the ones there now are not the ones who were there a few years ago. Most of them, says a former member, eventually are overpowered by their surroundings and have to return to places with more mortal scales and perspectives. But it is a great place to visit.

**Point Sur Light** 25 miles south of Monterey introduces the region. It looks like it is perched on a low, turtle-backed island, but a sandy causeway connects the hummock with the mainland. It is about the last undramatic moment in the Big Sur landscape.

Just south of it, the road begins to climb and to work its way inland for a time.

**Pfeiffer-Big Sur State Park** five miles south of the light, is the only camping park between Monterey and Morro Bay. It is a beautiful park, spread out across gently sloping hills, with shading redwoods in some places and open meadows in others. Its most-used feature is an impounded section of the Big Sur River, which forms a cool, naturally circulating swimming pool.

The park has no ocean frontage, but there are places to get down to the water nearby. One is just across the highway at the south side of the park. The owner of the property charges a fee for passage, and is the final arbiter of how many people go down to the shore.

Just south, State Highway 1 runs inland just a bit. It is in this region that the art colony shows itself to the passing public at any of several commercial establishments. Once past these, the road rejoins the sea and begins to gain altitude. It is no road for a certified acrophobe, because it is only a notch cut in the face of the cliffs, sometimes 1,100 feet above the water. The Grand Corniche in France doesn't get any higher, narrower, or more winding, and it doesn't have any more awesome panoramas.

**Jade Beach** is more than one beach. It, or they, are between the tiny towns of Lucia and Pacific Valley, 55 and 62 miles south of Monterey, respectively. It is possible to find real jade on the beach, although it is not of a quality to threaten treasures of the Ming Dynasty. The pieces are small, and beginning to be rare after years of rockhounds. Skin divers in the offshore waters do better. Fairly distinct trails lead down the bluffs from turnout points along the highway.

San Simeon is on down the highway, and is described in the preceding chapter.

# In gentle pursuit of tidepool animals

*In the tidepools,* a starfish dining, a sea anemone going hungry, a sea urchin at home

The whole notion of leaving a length of sandy beach to make a precarious trip across slippery rocks may seem foolish. It may even be foolish. But in the pools left behind by an ebbing tide there remain animals whose habits are a good deal more bizarre, or comic, or miraculous than any human swimmer's.

Looking at nature underfoot is diverting at least, and may even get to be engrossing in these communities between the tides. In fair warning it should be said, though, that tidepooling is a little bit like grand opera: It is more fun if the viewer knows the score. It also should be noted in advance that patience is a prime requisite. A good many of these animals exist without haste, and it may take an hour or more for one to do anything interesting.

Once the commitment is made to wait and watch, a tidepooler may see a starfish employ its very strange table manners. When eating a mussel, the starfish forces the two shells of its meal apart, then slips its reversible stomach inside the mussel shell and digests the luckless animal in its own home. Once finished the starfish retracts that aggressive stomach and glides away. It is easy to see when a meal is in progress. The starfish hunches over its dinner, rather than spreading out as it does in relaxed moments.

Another odd aspect of the starfish is its method of grooming. The entire skin surface is covered with tiny biting cells that take a nip out of anything that tries to rest on the starfish. These cells will grasp human hair if it comes in contact with them, and are strong enough to lift a hair out of place. This demonstration is entirely painless to both parties.

The starfish is one animal among thousands that live by the edge of the sea. Its habits are no more or less rare than those of sea anemones, sea urchins, crabs of all sorts, nudibranchs, or even barnacles.

Finding animals to look at is a matter of knowing something about their survival needs. The seashore provides a number of highly distinct environments, and most animals find all but one or two of them hostile. The main distinctions are in prevailing wave action, type of surface, and tide range. Many kinds of snails, clams, and worms prefer the quiet waters of bays. Some like muddy bottom. Others like clean sand. A very few animals thrive in the pounding of heavy surf on exposed sand beaches, the easiest to spot being Pismo and razor clams and the mole crab. But the greatest number of familiar animals like rocky places where the water becomes highly aerated by its splashing, and where the tide leaves both bright and dark places exposed when it ebbs. Some of the animals must stay in pools. Others can endure dry periods on bare rock. A rocky outcrop that is somewhat protected from the full onslaught of the waves is likely to have greater populations than a place that takes the full brunt of every passing wave. A place that has a flourishing colony of mussels is likely to have a good many more animals in the proximate neighborhood.

There are three tools every beginning tidepooler should acquire to further his pleasures in the hobby.

The first is a good field guide. One book is *Between Pacific Tides*, Third Edition, revised, by Ricketts and Calvin (Stanford Press, $6.95). The Ricketts in this case is the man who inspired the character Doc of *Cannery Row* by John Steinbeck. The book is a serious work of science, but the following short sample is typical of the prose: "If this spine (of an infant stage of a crab) has any function, it is, presumably, to make ingestion by enemies difficult. An enterprising pup that had just attacked its first porcupine would understand the principle involved." Or, "The (rock oyster) when young is not to be distinguished from a scallop. It swims in just the same way by flapping its two equal shells. But the ways of senile old age creep on it rapidly. The half-buried under surface of some great rock offers the appeal of a fireside nook to a sedentary scholar, and there it settles."

The second tool is a 10-power magnifying glass, because some of the best acts in this whole show are on the miniature side. The nudibranch, for example, wears brighter clothes than the average tropical fish. It can't be seen in its lemon yellows or scarlets without a good glass, being a shell-less snail hardly more than a quarter of an inch long.

The third tool, for the advanced amateur biologist or conchologist who goes hunting in bay shallows, is a look box that gets the glare off the water's surface and allows clear view of the bottom, where snail tracks are.

It is not good psychology to close with a sermon. However, the ranks of tidepool animals have been depleted so seriously in some areas that whole species threaten to disappear from view at any moment. Most of the depleting seems to have been done by people who had no idea that the animals they gathered would die in a matter of hours, would lose their colors and forms, would begin to smell foully soon after they die. Purposeful collecting is always done moderately, so the beaches will go on being interesting.

# San Francisco to Santa Cruz

San Franciscans and their suburban neighbors on the peninsula to the south enjoy a remarkable diversity of shore in the scant 80 miles that separate the city from Santa Cruz.

San Francisco is the Paris of the West to its admirers, a city by turns elegant, bawdy, traditional, new, cosmopolitan and provincial (but always for good cause). It is always a seaport and a crowded place.

Santa Cruz at the other end of the road is a carnival town with seasonal crowds but no great pressure of population—a town and not a city. Its summer weather is infinitely preferable to San Francisco's for outdoor swimming, picnicking, and strolling.

The space between is hardly populated at all. A couple of fishing villages south of San Francisco, then all is artichoke and brussels sprout fields, or brushy hillside.

The greater part of the shore is a narrow sand beach below steep sandstone bluffs. On these beaches, sunbathers, picnickers, surf fishermen, smelters, and walkers congregate in season. At the rocky outcrops, tidepoolers and rockhounds add their presence, and in a few locations the waves suit themselves to surfing. There are only three beaches in the whole skein safe for swimming, but then the water is cold enough that they are ample to the need.

Weather is the root cause of the differences between San Francisco's shore and that at Santa Cruz. The summer fog bank rolls ashore at San Francisco almost every day from June until September, and the daily maximum temperature is 64°. The fog doesn't get to Santa Cruz, where the temperatures get up to 75 as early as June, and peak at 77° as an average through August and September. (It is a trick of topography that the fog can more easily chase the warm air in the Central Valley through the Golden Gate.) San Francisco's winter high averages 57° as compared to 62° in Santa Cruz. Both places have superbly clear springs and falls. San Francisco's seawater temperature hovers between 53 and 57°. Santa Cruz has offshore shoals that produce local warming.

## Old San Francisco

A great deep sea port seldom has many people in it who think of the local shore as a recreation, mainly because port shores are usually littered with piers and begrimed with oil. In San Francisco the case is otherwise. There is plenty of open shore, and it is clean and attractive from the Golden Gate south to the county line.

### THE SAN FRANCISCO BEACHES

In crowded San Francisco it takes no effort to find hordes of gregarious souls on sandy, sun-warmed beach below the Great Highway. But, on most days of the year, the ocean shore is one of the best places in the city to seek solitude.

**Fort Point,** chill in the shadow of the Golden Gate Bridge, may not qualify as a beach in the whole sense of the word, but it is a favorite haunt for rock fishermen and a haunting reminder of a day when oceans were far more important in the national defense.

A seawall runs along beneath the decaying walls of the old Fort Winfield Scott. From it patient men try for striped bass and take whatever comes along. They cast and retrieve in the presence of a considerable array of historical ghosts, both maritime and military. The point has caught and wrecked its share of ships, among them the great clipper *Golden Fleece* which ran aground in an April storm in 1854 and began to destroy herself before a mob of weekend spectators (she was a tough old hull; she didn't break up altogether until late October), and the *Rio de Janeiro* which sank with 131 aboard in 1912. Assuming the treacherous waters of the gate wouldn't be enough to deter a resolute enemy, the Army in 1861 erected the fort so cannon could command the harbor entrance. With never an earnest shot, the fort closed down in 1914. Now airborne and amphibious invasion techiques leave very little reason to command harbor mouths. But the fort is a fine relic and placed to offer an extraordinary view of the gate, the bridge, the bay, and The City. To get to it, head west on Lincoln Boulevard from the Presidio Main Gate (Lombard and Baker) for a mile and three-fourths to the Fort Point turnoff sign on the north side of the road.

Weekends, guides in civil war uniforms conduct tours of the damp, cold insides of the fort. Visitors learn to be glad they were not in the old army before they head back out to watch fishermen ply their patient trade.

**Bakers Beach State Park,** just west of the bridge where the Golden Gate begins to belly out, draws heavy attendance from surf fishermen and inveterate bridge watchers, of which San Francisco has an abundance of each kind.

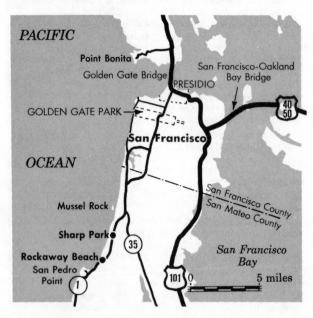

*SHORESIDE CAMPING: New Brighton State Park (100 units); Seacliff State Park (26 trailer units); Sunset Beach State Park (50 units), all south of Santa Cruz and north of Watsonville on Monterey Bay. SHORESIDE ACCOMMODATIONS: Santa Cruz has an abundance. No list available. Very sparse in San Francisco and San Mateo counties—a few in Pacifica, Princeton.*

*Sea wall* fishermen at Fort Point          *Surf fishermen* try their skills at Baker Beach

The fishing is reasonably good all year around, but the big striped bass go outside the gate mainly in July and August.

The most dramatic season for bridge-watching roughly coincides with the bass season. In summer, the big fog bank rolls in and out of the gate in its most theatrical form of the year, now swallowing up the great red bridge altogether, now nipping off the Marin County end, now covering the water but leaving the tops of the towers sticking up into a blue sky. It is worth dropping by two or three afternoons a week just to see how things are going in this brilliant panorama.

Baker Beach is at the foot of 25th Avenue.

**James D. Phelan Beach** resembles Baker Beach in most of its externals. The difference is that it has the only safe swimming of any of the San Francisco ocean beaches. There are lifeguards on duty, and surf fishermen are prohibited from using the shore between the hours of 10 a.m. and 6 p.m. in the summer. The beach also has picnic facilities.

The beach is at the foot of 40th Avenue.

Just southwest, the cliffs at Lands End beckon to the adventurous. San Francisco newspaperwoman Margot Patterson Doss summed up the collective past experience: "The lucky ones are taken off by helicopter. The others wind up with Mother Carey's chickens in the water below."

**The Great Highway** for three miles follows the back of the long, straight ocean beach that forms San Francisco's western boundary. Broad, sandy, and edged with notably cold and current-ridden water, the beach is used all year around by surf-fishermen, surfers, and neighborhood beach walkers. In sunny times (mainly spring and early fall), it

may hold swarms of people out for the simple pleasure of sunbathing next to a good, noisy surf.

Swimming is highly inadvisable. Shallow water and sand bars produce rip currents that can out-muscle most swimmers. Surf sometimes mounts unexpectedly, trapping innocent swimmers in water so turbulent that it literally pounds people against the bottom. And, finally, eccentric water temperatures prevail along this shore making the presence of sharks unpredictable. (The same great oceanic current that produces San Francisco's fog advances toward and retreats from the bay mouth area all willy nilly, alternately warming and cooling the water near shore. With warmer waters come dangerous sharks.)

Each year a great number of people who know better risk their lives attempting to save people who did not know enough. Even so, the list of lives lost along this beach is long.

The surfers who come here in spite of all the inclemencies of the local climate usually stay near the rocky headland, at the north end of the beach. They share the general neighborhood with a herd of sea lions whose main place of residence is the dome shaped rock just offshore from the Cliff House. Both surfers and sea lions reside in the area all year.

Midway along the Great Highway, Golden Gate Park comes down to the highway, a great swath of green between the amusement park north of it and the neat homes off to the south. At this edge of the park maritime buffs can take a look at the vessel Roald Amundsen used to explore seas much too big and storm-tossed for any such frail, wee craft. It sits beneath a sheltering roof just at the side of the road northbound.

Fleischhacker Zoo marks the southern terminus of the

# *Squidding for striped bass*

*Successful squidder* at Sharps Park—and a portrait of the striped bass

San Francisco Bay is still the largest population center of the West Coast's striped bass, and during the summer months many of them venture out through the Golden Gate and cause a flurry of surf-fishing activity along the coastal beaches.

Summer bass fishermen usually employ one of two surf-fishing methods: Bait fishing or squidding. The term squidding is derived from a metal squid that has been used as a surf lure along the Atlantic coast for many years. Variations on this lure are favorites on the ocean beaches of Marin, San Francisco, and San Mateo counties.

The ideal squidding situation occurs when stripers are feeding on such as anchovies close to shore. The presence of a school of bait fish is often heralded by a swoop of gulls or other fish-eating birds. A squidder will toss his lure wherever he sees a flock of birds, and some will drive up and down the coast for miles looking for this portent.

Casting a squid eliminates a need for sinkers, so lighter tackle can be used than is needed for bait casting. Most surf fishermen prefer a bait outfit so they can switch without a fight.

beach, down where the sand mounds into shifty dunes on Sand Dollar Beach.

## TWO LIVELY MUSEUMS

San Francisco harbors two museums which between them contain aspects of the sea for every man.

**San Francisco Maritime Museum** in one building and four ships spread out beyond each end of Fisherman's Wharf, takes in the whole romance between seafarers and this great port. Books, charts, models, and relics from vessels long since passed from the sea lanes fill the two stories of the main building next to Aquatic Park and across from Ghirardelli Square. A long block east, three ships moored at the foot of Hyde Street (below the Powell-Hyde cable car turn-around) are kept in mint condition. Tourists who come aboard can cast a wondering eye on how things must have been in the coastal trade from the turn of

the century, then can sample the romantic memory of the bay ferries. Clear off at the other side of Fisherman's Wharf, at Pier 43, the venerable three-master *Balclutha* tugs at her lines like she wanted to go somewhere. The uncomfortable truth is that the city seems a bit loathe to pay for her keep, and there is periodic talk that Los Angeles will take her away someday, owing to the fact that she is seaworthy and lacks only for a crew. While she is around she is fine to see and her tween decks are full of memories of the day of sail.

**Steinhart Aquarium** is the other institution of note to lovers of salt water. Located in the middle of Golden Gate Park in the Natural History museum complex, the Steinhart is one of the fine aquaria on the Pacific Coast. Most of the Pacific fishes are on view in tanks in the main exhibition hall, as are reptiles, amphibians, and some sea mammals.

For the beach lover, though, the main attraction will

be the remarkable tidepools that came out of the great remodeling of 1962. In these pools, wave machines set up a fair approximation of surf, and in addition to that the tide does indeed ebb and flood on a schedule identical to that the pool's inhabitants would expect. There are some intertidal invertebrates that refuse to put up with imitations, and there are more that tolerate the idea for only a few months. But, by and large, this device suits most of the creatures an average tidepool explorer might run across at the shore, and in surroundings that allow close and satisfying study of their appearances and habits.

Well, one qualification has to be made. Weekends, it is hard to get through the door, let alone next to one of the displays. Best time is a fiercely rainy morning in midweek.

## San Mateo coast

Nearly all of the 50 plus mile San Mateo County coastline is publicly accessible, and nearly all of the accessible beach is within San Mateo State Beaches parkland.

One dramatic headland of steep rock between Pacifica and Moss Beach gives motorists a chance to drive on some cliff-hanging highway before State 1 settles down to the business of getting people across rolling coast hills at a good pace. A homogenous terrain of brush-covered hills extends from Montara to the south county line. Rocky outcroppings are a rarity. The shore is mainly a narrow sandy beach below soft sandstone bluffs that range from a few feet to more than 100 feet in height. Few towns reach down to the shore, and after Half Moon Bay there is none until Santa Cruz.

### SAN MATEO STATE BEACHES

San Mateo State Beaches comes in a flock of small parcels all with a basic similarity, each with a quality of its own. The summer crowds are sizable.

**Thornton Beach State Park,** the northernmost segment of San Mateo Beaches, lies just below the San Francisco county line, almost adjoining the Olympic Country Club. It is a tough one-mile hike from the end of the road, which leads west from State 1 just south of the county line.

**Sharp Park Beach State Park,** six miles south on the seaward side of Sharp Park public golf course, is similar. The wide sandy beach backed by rolling dunes offers few amenities, and is isolated enough to make for good beach walking. It also marks the southern end of the good surf fishing for striped bass. A few of the big fish get farther south, but not in worthwhile numbers.

**Montara Beach State Park** heaves into view as State 1 corkscrews back down toward sea level from its giddy peak of 700 feet altitude. The park area, like most of the others, is sand at the foot of sandstone bluffs. What lies south of the park offers diversion from that diet. Montara Light adjoins the beach on the south, its squat structure perched on the north edge of an outcropping of rock that extends to become the famous tidepool area of Moss Beach.

Moss Beach, alas, is something of a has-been in the tide-

*Historic coast vessels moored at foot of Hyde St.*

*Princeton-by-the-Sea, an active fishing village*

pooling trade. Several score generations of young biology students have collected their first intertidal invertebrates from these celebrated rocks, with the net result that very few living things remain, not counting the students. Divers do pretty well locally, even with the ever-scarcer abalone, once below the tide zone.

**Half Moon Bay State Beach Park** lies halfway between the towns of Half Moon Bay and Princeton-by-the-sea, and in the shadow of an aging pink hotel at Miramar. The beach is of coarse sand of the kind used by heartless college football coaches to strengthen the legs and lungs of their charges on the theory that running in such jelly-like substance will make running on firm turf a joy by comparison.

Surfers, surf-fishermen, and sunbathers use this beach in season. The surfing is frequently of the proper sort for apprentices, a steady series of three or four foot waves advancing toward a wide beach uncluttered by rocks or other complications. It is the only beach along this coast safe for swimming.

Off to the north low, sandy Pillar Point protects this beach from the full onslaught of Pacific waves, and provides the base for the breakwater-protected small boat harbor at Princeton. Commercial and sportfishing vessels operate out of this unexpectedly Mediterranean village. Its main street is proportionately fishy, with both restaurants and fish stalls contributing to the flavor.

A spur road, well marked, goes from State 1 directly into the commercial street of Princeton. Just south of it, a loop road cuts west from the highway across grassy fields and through the scattering of buildings that is Miramar.

**Dunes Beach State Park** adjoins this general area on the south and is much like it. The only facilities at the shore end of a plainly signed, half-mile spur road, are the standard park restrooms. It is possible to walk along the beach from one park to the other.

**San Gregorio State Beach Park** is the next developed park beach. It, like its neighbors north and south, has only restrooms. San Gregorio lies eight and-a-half miles south of the town of Half Moon Bay and is separated from it by a fairly lofty if round-shouldered hill. The beach itself is the edge of a small alluvial plain engineered by San Gregorio Creek. The creek meanders through the beach sand in summer, pausing in a shallow lagoon that warms quickly when the sun shines so children can splash and wade in greater comfort here than almost anywhere else along this stretch of coast. Headlands north and south baffle the wind at least partially, which adds to the beach's desirable qualities as a spot for family picnics.

The north headland is impassable at high tide, but the beachwalker can stroll for miles to the south if he has a mind to do so. (He can in summer, anyway. In winter the surf can get up high enough to make the journey unsafe.) The beach south is backed by a high, steep sandstone bluff. An odd effect of the bluff is that it traps and reflects the considerable sound of the surf, so that the end result is a deep-throated, one-noted, interminable roar which makes the rest of the world seem oddly quiet after a day on the beach. The bluff also produces upwelling breezes that benefit seagulls no end. The birds cruise along the rim of the bluffs without effort until something below catches their ceaselessly hungry attention. Then they swoop down in matchless displays of aerobatic ease.

*San Gregorio Beach offers miles of strolling room*

Rangers in jeeps patrol the length of the beach, keeping an eye on the general conduct of the crowds as well as the welfare of surfers and waders.

Of course open coast, sandy beaches like this one and its neighbors support only a very few life forms. The commonest along here is the sand crab, or mole crab, a scuttling armadillo of a creature that spends its entire life swimming, digging, and walking backwards. Its prime enemies are sandpipers and small boys, both of which exist abundantly. Seashells are less common than beer cans, tennis shoes, and cull fruits from adjoining artichoke farms. In compensation, rubble from the sandstone bluffs can be picked at to find fossil shells, or shells in the process of becoming fossils. Big chunks of the sandstone break loose because of wind and spray pressure on the bluff face. Almost every boulder-sized one of these will yield at least one impression of a shell. (It pays, incidentally, to keep out from under the brow of these bluffs. Chunks come down on an irregular schedule, and every once in a while a really impressive slide takes place.)

**Pescadero Beach State Park** some four and-a-half miles south of San Gregorio, resembles the latter in that it occupies the alluvial fan of a small creek. It differs in having several rocky tongues that stick out to sea, forming both tidepools and some picturesque surf.

Both this beach and San Gregorio draw great crowds on sunny days. They are close enough to San Francisco and the suburban towns of the Peninsula that the word of sun gets around quickly. Still and all, the wide sandy spaces are difficult to fill. There always seems to be elbow room at the price of a stroll up or downcoast from the

*Pigeon Point*, a good place for tidepoolers, skin divers, and lighthouse buffs

parking lots which in each case are large ones.

The diversions at this beach parallel those at San Gregorio. In spite of the rocky areas, tidepool exploring has long since ceased to be especially productive.

**Pebble Beach State Park** occupies a sandy cove hemmed in at north and south by outcrops of rock. The beach is two and-a-half miles south of Pescadero (about 45 miles south of San Francisco), and owes its fame to the particular beauty of the pebbles that the sea chips out of the rock mass and casts up on shore. The hues of these stones are particularly delicate and captivating to the feminine eye. Clear back in 1893 a Mrs. C. F. Wilson of Pescadero built a three-foot-high model of Pigeon Point Light using these stones, and displayed it at the Columbian Exposition in Chicago, Illinois. Since then Mrs. Wilson's like-minded successors have eroded the supply of stones sufficiently to cause the state to place an embargo on further collecting.

The embargo has not succeeded completely. One compensatory result of the stones' beauty is that few people pay much attention to the animals in the fine tidepools here.

**Arroyo de los Frijoles Beach State Park,** another mile south, resembles Pebble Beach closely and is the end of the state park.

## PIGEON POINT AND ANO NUEVO

The park ends before the county coastline does. It is on this southern nub that two of its most distinctive shore areas await their few admirers.

**Pigeon Point Light** exemplifies lighthouse architecture.

The slim, graceful tower painted white looms above the shelf of rock on which it was built in all haste after the clipper ship *Carrier Pigeon* (hence the name) went aground here during a storm on the night of June 6, 1853. All hands were got ashore safely, but Captain Azariah Doane's $54,000 ship was a complete loss.

Aside from the photogeniety of the lighthouse, this is a diverting few hundred yards of shore. The usual low, sandstone bluff prevails north of the point for some distance, but a variety of rocks project into the sea from this bank. These produce some fine tidepools (the rocks are bedded in nearly level planes) with preponderant communities of green anemones and hermit crabs in between the mussel beds. The rocks and shoals extend offshore far enough to generate some theatrical surf, too. Finally, the odd mixture of an almost black sandstone with buff conglomerate will give visiting rockhounds and amateur geologists points for conjecture. Piddocks, fairly abundant here, have created and abandoned some strangely sculpted small rocks to add to hunting possibilities. A stretch of sand beach borders this to the north.

South of the light station, more rocks partially sheltered by the point make good hunting grounds for skin divers.

Summer weekends from 1 to 4 p.m. adults in street attire are eligible to tour the light station. Children are permitted only if accompanied by an adult. There is no admittance to the tower, where 1,008 pieces of polished glass make up a lens which beams light 18 miles out to sea, as it has since the station went into operation in 1872.

**Point Ano Nuevo State Reserve** lies almost athwart the

# In hardy pursuit of smelt

*There are several ways to catch smelt: 2-man net, A-frame dip net, or smelt rakes*

The west's true smelt (*Osmeridae*) run the summer surf from Alaska's chilly gulf waters as far south as Point Conception in California, and wherever the smelt run, smelt fishermen are sure to follow.

The tasty little fish (fry them in deep fat, cleaned but with heads and tails intact) grow to a 7 to 10-inch size, and spawn in shallow tidewater. The regulations governing sportfishing for them vary from state to state along the coast. It is always best to check locally about the legality of gear, closed seasons, and limits (25 pounds, or a regular galvanized bucket full in most cases).

The best beaches for smelt seem to have two common characteristics. They are sandy, and below bluffs from which fresh water seeps down into the beach area.

Smelt generally come to the edge of the water about when a tide is changing (either an hour before a high tide or an hour after). Swarming gulls often mark a school of smelt while the fish are still 50 to 100 yards offshore.

The simplest way to catch the fish is with a smelt rake, in effect a semi-cylindrical net mounted on a rectangular frame with a long handle. In calm water, it is a fairly simple matter to scoop through a receding wave with a long stroke that cups the fish in the net. These rakes are unwieldy in running surf, so are mainly popular in Puget Sound.

The 6-foot dip net on an A-frame gets the widest use of any method. All it takes is skill, courage and enough physical strength to stand up to rolling surf. The fisherman plants his net with the wide end of the A down, lets the wave surge past, then holds the net to catch smelt riding the backwash out to sea. A good man with one of these can take two waves, holding the first catch in one fold as he makes the second catch. It takes a lot of practice.

Yet a third method, legal and popular from San Francisco to the south side of Monterey County, is the two-man net. It can be as long as 20 feet, and has to have a 7/8-inch mesh. A pole at each end gives it shape. In this case, one man at each end maneuvers the net to catch a backwash, then the two together struggle up the beach face with (they hope) a bulky burden. This is an easier trick to master than the A-frame net, but it takes just as much muscle.

Some of the best-known smelt beaches along the coast are Kalaloch and Ruby Beach in Washington, Bastendorff (Coos Bay) and Yachats in Oregon, and Westport and San Gregorio in California.

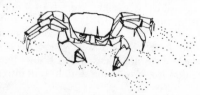
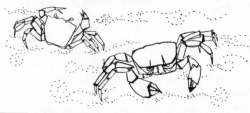

*Few **tourists** can resist a short stroll to the rock arches at Natural Bridges State Park*

San Mateo-Santa Cruz county line. A long, curving sand beach follows the inside arc of the point. The offshore island at the tip of the point is a reserve for sea lions and sea birds.

Not many people use it for a variety of reasons.

First, it is not clearly marked. A scattering of ranch buildings on the seaward side of the road six miles south of Pigeon Point is the clue for an approaching driver to slow down for a narrow spur road that leads off at right angles. Parking along this road is sparse and is, furthermore, a mile from the point which can be reached only by slogging through soft, coarse sand.

Second, the prevailing westerly winds howl around the arc, aimed by a steep bluff behind the narrow beach. The winds pose their own discomfort, and abet it by sweeping up stinging sheets of sand and hurling them against any exposed skin in sight.

Third, in summer hundreds of stinging jellyfish (Velella, commonly mis-identified as Portuguese Man O'Wars) drift into the protected water inside the point.

No chamber of commerce would admit having a place like that, but in spite of everything the beach is busy day after day all summer with surfers (the learner's permit type mainly), picnickers, and readers of Russian novels and other weighty literature. Most of them bring wind shelters and wood for open picnic fires. Not a few bring sturdy kites to fly in the brisk onshore-offshore winds. (The cheap, store-boughten variety will disintegrate in no time at all. Heavy duty homemades with butcher paper are the ticket.)

## SANTA CRUZ OCEAN BEACHES

Santa Cruz County does not present much of its coastline to the open ocean, but what there is is unusual and in places dramatic.

**Natural Bridges Beach State Park** just north of the city of Santa Cruz and accessible from either State Highway 1 or by West Cliff Drive, can divert the visitor in several ways: scenery watching, tidepool exploring, swimming, or picnicking.

The natural bridges themselves—one collapsed, two standing, one building—are wave-caused perforations in a long, thin, curving finger of hard sandstone that emerges, mysteriously, from a hillock of softer stuff.

To the south, high rock bluff fronts on the sea and gives incoming waves good excuse to work themselves into a froth. To the north of the bridges, beyond a deep cove of sand, the rock takes over again. In the latter case, there is at the foot of a steep bluff an extensive shelf.

This shelf of almost level rock holds within its cradling shape dozens of fine tidepools, some of the best in the region. Students come here, but in fewer numbers than they visit Moss Beach, so intertidal animals are still present in sufficient numbers for a mildly inquiring pair of eyes to uncover a representative or two of each of the common species along this cold water coast.

The sandy cove between bridges and bluff is several hundred feet across and almost as deep. Nearly level, its clean, drift-free surface sparkles white under a summer sun. Swimmers and air mattress riders find the surf ideal

*Greyhound Rock*, *a choice spot for rock fishing*

*Miss California* *hopefuls at Santa Cruz boardwalk*

for their purposes. Full-fledged, board-riding surfers get better action at beaches inside Monterey Bay.

Behind the cove, in scrub pines that mount up a gentle slope toward the park entrance, 25 picnic sites get good play on every warm day.

**Scott Creek,** 12 miles north of Santa Cruz (2 miles north of the sand mill at Davenport), is the next point of public beach access along the coast. It is not a park. A rough spur road drops down to beach level from State 1. Surf fishing is the prime lure, here, at the mouth of a small creek canyon.

It would seem that a veritable army of people have tried to expand upon the amount of open beach north of Santa Cruz, where most of the coastal shelf is planted to brussels sprouts. Enough people have tried, anyway, to cause some local farmers to put up curt signs, like "No trespassing. Don't ask."

**Greyhound Rock,** a long beach area set aside by the county specially for fishermen, lies 18 miles north of Santa Cruz at the foot of a towering bluff. The big name-sake rock in the tide zone comes into a driver's view at about the same time he sees a small sawmill perched on a headland just to the north of the beach area. A super-market sized parking lot on the seaward side of the road attests to the popularity of a place that, bluntly, should be popular with any man with a touch of the martyr in his soul. From the parking lot, a narrow path plummets steeply down 150 feet of bluff face to a beach of sand so coarse that even waves do not compact it. Greyhound Rock itself is only a few feet from the foot of the path, but more than half a mile to the south a shelf of rock jutting out from the bluff into the surf zone attracts more

locally knowledgeable types.

Tidepooling is fair along that bluff.

**Waddell Creek Beach,** just south of the San Mateo county line, 20 miles from Santa Cruz, forms the mouth of a surprisingly sizable creek canyon, the fertile bottom of which is picturesque farm. The sign by the road says no fishing at this beach, which is long, straight and sandy. State 1 cuts along behind the beach almost at sea level. There are turnouts every few feet for almost a mile.

## MONTEREY BAY BEACHES

Monterey, around on the south side of the bay, is vacation country in one sense. The Santa Cruz County half of the Monterey Bay shoreline is vacation country in a different sense, but a complementary one.

Monterey capitalizes on its romantic Spanish tradition and the awesome ruggedness of its seascapes. Santa Cruz capitalizes on a tinsel and glitter carnival and the presence of good swimming beaches by the mile. Monterey seeks and gets the convention trade with fine restaurants and exclusive shops, elegant hostelries and toney golf courses. Santa Cruz seeks and gets the family trade with top-drawer camping parks, thousands of privately-owned beach cottages that rent by the week and month, and all that safe, warm swimming beach.

**Santa Cruz Beach,** the municipal strand below the carnival boardwalk, draws thousands of young families and teen-agers who drive down for a day in the sun on any day from June 15 to Labor Day, and who then retreat through gathering dusk to any town inland in the hot coastal valleys. The swimming is good. Sometimes the surfing is fair at the south end of the beach by a small lagoon.

*Sand engineers* at Seacliff State Park

And there is always the razz-matazz of the boardwalk, which sports one of the best merry-go-rounds in existence among its other rides and games.

In summer the most attractive and virtually the only shore life is human. The attractiveness hits an early peak in June when the Miss California Pageant takes place on the boardwalk pier. After Labor Day, though, the crowds thin steadily and it is not long before even a warm evening sees the beach deserted save for a woman walking her dog toward ever-retreating flocks of sandpipers.

The boardwalk goes to a weekends-only schedule.

At the west edge of the public beach, a long pier points south. At its outer end are sportfishing boats (bottom fishing mainly), restaurants, and small boys with handlines.

**Twin Lakes State Beach** is on East Cliff Drive at the South city limits of Santa Cruz. Two lagoons back the shoreline, which is several thousand feet long, and headlands close off the beach at either end. All of this plus the presence of a small boat moorage makes this park one of the most popular in the area. Several local buslines serve the park.

**Capitola State Beach,** 3½ miles east of Santa Cruz, off State 1 at the mouth of Soquel Creek, serves the same sort of function as Twin Lakes. The city of Capitola maintains a freshwater swimming pool next to the creek mouth as an alternative to the colder, rougher bay water. Good surf fishing exists here.

**New Brighton State Beach,** a 65 acre park split between upland meadow and sandy beach, has 90 campsites, the first camping park on the coast south of the Golden Gate. This fact alone tends to make it a favorite weekend destination for families with children. Its general usefulness as a family park is enhanced by protecting headlands

that make swimming safe even for youngsters while they add to the variety of shore fishing. The campsites are in the high meadows, from where panoramic views out to the bay have a rare serenity on soft summer evenings when the fog stays well offshore.

A sign on State 1, four miles east of Santa Cruz, marks the access road to the park.

**Seacliff State Beach** used to be a camping park, but has developed into a day-use park that draws crowds of a density unparalleled elsewhere north of Los Angeles.

Its two miles of ocean frontage offer what park officials describe as the safest ocean swimming in the state. It like all other segments of this great, curving bay has broad sandy beach mounding slowly up from the tide zone, a prime asset for the thousands who come here to bask in the sun (and this park marks the end of the least foggy stretch of coast in Central California. Santa Cruz is the northern terminus.) Another prime factor leading to the park's annual attendance of 1,000,000 is the fishing pier, a great long thing extended by a 435-foot concrete ship called the *Palo Alto* in her brief sailing days. The mis-named vessel was built during World War I, towed to the area and sunk in the 1920's, and broken in two by winter storms since. But her after section can still be boarded by fisherman after perch, kingfish, sole, flounder, halibut, tomcod, jacksmelt, lingcod, cabezon and an infrequent salmon or steelhead. It can also be boarded by children in quest of the crabs that lurk in the ventilator wells. A concessioner operates in the park, the main drawback of which is inadequate parking.

Access to Seacliff is marked on State 1 by signs for the beach community of Aptos, which strings out along the top of the bluffs behind the beach.

**Manresa State Beach,** undeveloped at this time, serves surf fishermen and clammers. The surf fishermen go after the same quarry as their counterparts at Seacliff, but without the convenience of a pier. Clammers can dig a limit of Pismos, if they have persistence.

Access is from State 1, 10 miles north of Watsonville. Posted signs point the way.

**Sunset State Beach,** four miles due west of Watsonville via one of the town's main cross streets, along with New Brighton serves the needs of campers. Foggier conditions here inhibit swimming but do not prohibit it entirely. The surf is safe enough for the purpose. Aside from its greater number of amenities, Sunset's main audience is out for the same purpose as visitors to Manresa: surf fishing and Pismo clams (the season on the latter is from September through April). In addition to its 50 campsites, this park has picnic facilities amid the pleasant surroundings of pine, cypress, or eucalyptus trees planted in groves, atop the high bluff behind the beach, and surrounded by meadows that bloom profusely with poppies and bush lupines in March and April.

This park, with three and a half miles of beach front, is adjoined directly on the south by Palm Beach Park, which extends the shore area to seven miles, but which has yet to be developed. The park stops at the Pajaro river mouth.

Just south of the Pajaro River, in Monterey County, the undeveloped Zmudowski State Beach attracts surf fishermen in numbers. So does the equally undeveloped Salinas River Beach Park just south of Moss Landing.

# Golden Gate to Mendocino

Across from San Francisco, the Golden Gate headlands loom steep and rocky when the summer fog leaves them visible for inspection. They are an acceptably exaggerated advertisement for the coasts of Marin, Sonoma, and Mendocino counties, which are in the main steep and rocky and shrouded in summer fog.

The population of the coast is not at all intense in the more than 200 miles from the Golden Gate to the northern boundary of Mendocino, partly because the area has few uses in the contemporary industrial economy of California, and partly because the weather is less abrasive to human spirit just a few miles inland on the lee slopes of the coast hills.

Sheep, a few scattered lumber mills, and even fewer fishing harbors provide the main occupational employments in the region (as opposed to orchards, vineyards, and commute communities east of the ridges). For visitors, the prime charms are stubborn and even cranky survivors of earlier times. These include rambling old inns, some carpenter's Gothic architecture, a part-steam railroad known as the Skunk and operating between Fort Bragg and Willits, and a shore-hugging road that has suffered only minor improvements at the hands of function-minded highway engineers.

It is a great place to go sit in front of fireplaces with a supply of good books to read between trips out into an often cold, wet, and windy world where tidepooling and drift hunting are open to fitful interest, or where shore-fishing, abaloning, deep sea fishing, or skin diving require more serious effort.

In the several bays, clamming is possible.

## The Marin beaches

As far as mariners are concerned, the Pacific shore from Point Reyes to the Golden Gate has very little to recommend it. It is, for them, a venomous collection of sea fogs, howling winds, reefs, and shoals. But for the shorebound it is something else: Good fishing, good tidepooling, good rockhounding, and, in its shallow bays, good swimming, and some of central California's best shellfish country.

There is entertaining history connected to it, too.

**Point Bonita**, which forms the north tip of the Golden Gate, has on its eroding tip one of California's notably colorful lighthouses.

This is a prime weather station and warning point for the bay because it is a reliable checkpoint for the comings and goings of the summer fog bank. (This fog doesn't come and go on little kittens' feet, either. It comes and goes on a wind that roars like a lion.) The first sounding device installed here in 1856 to help be-fogged mariners grope through the Gate was chosen without sufficient statistical research. He was an Army sergeant who was charged with firing a muzzle-loading cannon at half hour intervals whenever the conditions required. He got food rations and a cottage in addition to his Army pay, and may have thought he had a good thing until he arrived on the job. At the end of two months the man was exhausted, and had to petition for relief. An unearthly electronic racket does the job now.

The light is closed to visitors these days, but its usefulness can be assessed from various vantages along the headlands.

**Golden Gate Headlands State Park,** although undeveloped except for a lofty, looping road, looks at development on all sides: west to the light, east to the Golden Gate Bridge and through the bridge to San Francisco.

Spring kite-flying and flower-watching is superb. There is one pocket beach near the bridge end of the park.

To get to the headlands, exit from U.S. 101 at the Sausalito turnoff just north of the bridge. Two hundred yards later a sign points left for Forts Baker, Barry and Cronkhite. The road goes through a tunnel and five miles on to Cronkhite Beach. Two miles beyond the tunnel a spur road leads left toward the light station. It connects with the cliff-hanging headland road.

**Fort Cronkhite** is the outermost of three sentinel forts on the north side of the Golden Gate, and the only one with publicly accessible beaches. The reasons for visiting may be several. Rockhounds enjoy the trip because the sandy strand usually has jadeite or jasper pebbles scattered along it, especially in winter. People who like to watch seabirds fly have here a constant supply, either

*SHORESIDE CAMPING: None. SHORESIDE ACCOMMODATIONS: Stinson Beach, Inverness, Marshall. No list available.*

*Cronkhite Beach offers birdwatching and rock hounding all year and sunbathing in summer*

on the offshore nesting rocks, or huddled in the lee of soft sandstone bluffs that were the beach in another geologic age. Sunbathers get protection from the westerlies from these same bluffs, and they show up in numbers when the weather is good enough for the sea birds to patrol over open water. Its remoteness—five miles from the Sausalito turnoff—does not inhibit summer crowds at all.

**Stinson Beach,** town and day-use state park, is the first place State 1 gets down to sea level after a twisting trip from U.S. 101 across Marin County hills of surpassing scenic worth, especially to people who have a lingering fondness for aged farmhouses set against forested hillsides and grassy valleys.

Stinson Beach, the park, parallels the road southeast of the town. It has several rocky points toward its east end that serve ideally for rock fishermen after perch, rock and ling cod, cabezones, and blennies. (Rocky Point and, farther east, Gull Rock are especially favored.) It has a fine swimming beach closer to town. The water, if not exactly tepid, registers several degrees warmer than the general summer water temperature around the Gate because of the extensive shoals of Bolinas Bay. Colder water and stronger currents make off-season swimming a risk.

This park attracts more than half-a-million visitors each summer, but the fact that the beach extends as a spit for three miles beyond the park means that there is always room enough for one more.

A road goes out to the tip of the spit, which on its ocean side has the same clean sand as the park beach. On the Bolinas Lagoon side, the bottom is muddier, a fact which permits the presence of some diverse clamming.

Cockles (the kind that come steamed in buckets) and Gapers (also known variously as horse and Empire clams) are the most abundant. The beds are depleted enough that it is a rarely skilled clammer who can dig a limit.

**Bolinas,** a wee small town on the opposite side of the lagoon from Stinson Beach, cannot be accused of courting tourists. It has few accommodations for them, but still people come in numbers to spend a day surfing, surf fishing for striped bass or lesser game, clamming, or hunting for rocks along Duxbury Reef.

The stripers tend to congregate in season at the mouth of Bolinas Lagoon. At the southwest corner of Bolinas, a county park at the end of the main street gives access to a raft of fine tidepools. In the sandy pockets between rocks, rockhounds find agates from time to time. A little farther west at a beach reached by way of a county road from Bolinas, the rock fishing is notably good.

All of these cheerfully innocent activities take place on the seaward side of Duxbury Reef, which sticks its semi-submerged snout out to sea from the town.

The north ship channel runs close in to shore from Bolinas because of Potato Patch shoal, a freakishly shaped bar that covers a wide arc across the north approach to the Golden Gate. This north channel, called Bonita Channel, passes along the Fort Cronkhite Beach, and to get into it a ship has to skirt Duxbury Reef close enough to avoid the Potato Patch. Modern navigation is refined enough to take most of the risk out of it, but in the days before radar a skipper had a hellish problem on his hands when the weather was up, which it usually was. An uncounted number of vessels have come to grief on the harsh rocks, most of them inconsequential to the large eye of history.

*Broad sweeping* cove forms Stinson Beach

**Point Bonita** Lighthouse and weather station

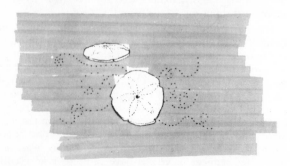

## POINT REYES PENINSULA

United States Weather Bureau statistics cede to Point Reyes the twin honors of foggiest and windiest station, bar none, between Canada and Mexico. But the point is only one outcropping of rock in a magnificently rumpled landscape, and its weather differs considerably from the gentler stuff at Inverness 11 miles away on Tomales Bay.

Natural history takes other unusual turns on this peninsula, and even a few unique ones. Human history has its rare moments as well. Withal, a long and diverse shoreline shows few signs of human occupation. All of these factors led to the area's being named Point Reyes National Seashore on September 5, 1962.

The peninsula's odd shape leaves it with three watery sides, each distinct from the others.

**Drake's Bay,** a long and gentle curve facing almost due south, has a wide, flat sandy beach abutting steep bluffs of soft sandstone from Point Reyes on the west to a point just above Bolinas on the east. The one break in the arc is the mouth of Drakes Estero, a clutching hand that sticks far into the middle of the peninsula, that cups oyster beds in its palm, and that may or may not have protected England's grand old freebooter Sir Francis Drake while his *Golden Hinde* was careened for repairs in 1579.

Drake's Beach County Park, reached by the Sir Francis Drake Highway from Inverness, has at the inland edge of its parking lot, a granite cross erected by one history society to commemorate the landing of Drake in the nearby estero.

The society has contended long since that Drake's log describes terrain and gives other evidence that this is the place. Other societies hold or have held for Bodega, Bolinas, Sausalito, and Half Moon Bay, all on the same evidence. The proponents for Sausalito argue that if Drake did indeed get into what is now Richardson Bay, he would replace Spaniard Gaspar de Portola as the discoverer of San Francisco Bay, and would move the date ahead by 190 years. In one sense it hardly matters because Drake made no great note of his findings on his return to England, and the British government did not act upon what he did say. Spain did act upon Portola's discovery. Yet, it is always good to have the record straight, and anyway this is a dandy academic argument that became even more spirited after the finding near Sausalito in 1937 of Drake's Plate of Brass. The plate, now on display in Bancroft Library on the University of California campus in Berkeley, is authentic. It matches in every respect the description of its placing written into the log of the voyage. It has passed metallurgical tests, too.

Whether the argument is solved by some dramatic new turn, or is never settled, Drakes Bay will go on being a pleasant place to amble away a long summer's day.

The old county park area was spruced up during the summer of 1965 and provides the main access point to the sandy stretch. Off to the east, about half way between the park and the estero mouth, several long, flat fingers of rock stick out into the water. The rocks, criss-crossed by what appear to be fossilized mud cracks, harbor a few marine invertebrates in small tidepools and at the same time induce eddies that seem to catch considerable drift. A fair number of shells wash up around them with each morning tide.

Westward of the parking area, along more protected waters, the backside of the rock outcropping that forms Point Reyes makes beachwalking tougher, and tide-pooling more rewarding.

There is a handsomely designed National Seashore visitor center alongside the parking lot. Within, it holds a set of dressing rooms, an office and bookstall, and a couple of sheltered places to sit and watch waves when the weather gets too raw to stay outdoors.

Beautifully symmetrical plunging breakers cream ashore in this bay, plumes of white spray flying above their crests when strong winds whistle across the lowlands from the ocean beaches to the northwest.

**Point Reyes**, rocks all atumble and 612 feet high, keeps visitors from staying on the shore when they leave Drake's Bay in favor of Point Reyes Beach.

The light station up on the point is now closed to visitors; alas, because the altitude provides sweeping views south beyond Bolinas town (its buildings hidden in a fold of hills), and north along the ruler-straight 12 miles of Point Reyes Beach. Ah, well. Most days are foggy, anyway.

In any season, wear a hat with a chin strap on the ocean side of the peninsula. The sea wind likely will blow gusts up to 40 miles per hour any day of the year. Close to the point, its fury seems to redouble.

**Point Reyes Beach,** steep-faced and current ridden, exposed to the scouring winds, and backed by low dunes or rolling hills, has a certain haunting charm about it. It hasn't much appeal to activists. Swimming is impossible and so is surfing. Surf fishing is not productive. Tidepools hardly exist.

To picnic, it is necessary to find or erect some kind of shelter unless wind-blown sand is to permeate the meal.

What this beach offers is solitude in terrain that looks like it should be lonely, and a chance to look for drift for 12 straight miles. That, 40 miles from San Francisco, is an advantage worth seeking now and again.

The other thing it offers, especially in winter, is astonishingly high surf. There are no offshore bars here to temper waves before they arrive on the beach. Sometimes big waves roll up from distant storms during the spell of freakishly warm weather that comes nearly every February. Odd thought though it is, picnicking is perfect then.

Several large parking lots on the seaward side of Sir Francis Drake Boulevard facilitate the launching of such expeditions.

**McClure's Beach,** on a fine day in September when other beaches for miles around seethe with relaxing folk, might be deserted. From Inverness, it is eight-plus miles out Pierce Point Road to a parking area, and from the parking area it is a twisty half mile walk down a ravine to the beach. There, the visitor gets a little of each of the aspects he might find by touring the rest of the peninsula's open beaches. The offshore rocks churn up a boiling froth. The wind blows tossing manes of spray above incoming breakers. Pocket beaches of sand offer the sun-bather a chance to stretch out. Picnickers find shelter behind drift logs or in the lee of rocks or bluffs. Abalone hunters do pretty well among the craggy rocks north of the beach

*Rocks* off McClure's Beach invite big breakers

*Sand-wiches* are always on the beach picnic menu

*Inverness Ridge* shelters Heart's Desire Beach

proper. The beds begin a half mile north of the beach and extend the rest of the way to Tomales Point. This is private land, and can be used only along the beach between the tidelines. Other tidepool creatures abound here as well, although collecting is prohibited because of the park status.

**Tomales Bay State Park** still identifies the string of pleasant little coves just north of the town of Inverness, although this area too falls within the National Seashore boundaries.

These beaches offer a marked contrast to the nearby ocean strands: Happily warm and quiet bay water where children can swim or anybody at all can fish from the shore, with plenty of room to picnic at tables sheltered under trees on the lee side of Inverness Ridge.

Tomales Bay is one of California's rewards for putting up with the San Andreas Fault's occasional binges of earthquake destruction. The fault runs in a true line through Bolinas Lagoon, along State Highway 1, then right up the floor of Tomales Bay. Point Reyes Peninsula is the cumulative result of activity along the fault. Inverness Ridge is the high side of the slip, and Tomales Bay the low. The peninsula is sometimes called an Island in Time because the rocks which form it have migrated to their present location from far south, and are unrelated to the rocks on the east side of the fault. This migration continues to inch northward. The vegetative cover and animal life on the peninsula differ markedly from counterpart life on the other side of the fault valley because Inverness Ridge causes a micro-climate variation so extreme that many plants and animals cannot endure the change from peninsula to mainland. The Bishop pine flourishes on the peninsula, but does not appear on the adjacent mainland.

The park beaches, south to north, are Shell, Pebble, Heart's Desire, and Indian. Entry to the park is from Pierce Point Road (the one that goes out to McClure's Beach). The south fork of the entrance road goes to a parking area for Shell Beach. The north fork leads to the other beaches. The park as a whole is a preserve for the Bishop pine, and a memorial grove of the trees is dedicated to pioneer botanist-conservationist Willis Linn Jepson.

## TOMALES BAY EAST SHORE

State Highway 1 follows the east shore of Tomales Bay with close fidelity from Point Reyes Station as far as the mouth of Walker Creek, then cuts inland to Tomales. From Tomales, the Dillon Beach Road cuts west through rolling meadowland to the shore at the mouth of the bay, while State 1 maunders along inland until the town of Bodega.

**Marshall,** population 50, sits about midway along the east shore of Tomales Bay, at the north end of a fair bed of cockles. Like Inverness across the way, it harbors a good number of small boats, mainly used to fish for striped bass and silver salmon in their respective seasons, and perch all year around. (Sharks and skates lurk on the bottom and are sought for the sport of it.) Several boat works stretch northward from Marshall, with attendant summer cabins.

**Dillon Beach** is a commercial establishment. At the bay mouth, it offers clamming, salmon, bass, halibut, and bottom fishing, and crabbing. There are fees for all of this.

*SHORESIDE CAMPING: Sonoma Beaches State Park (Wrights Beach section) (30 units). SHORESIDE ACCOMMODATIONS: Bodega Bay, Jenner, a few isolated inns along highway. Not numerous anywhere. No list available.*

A colony of trim summer homes occupies a hill to the north of the main beach area. The houses crowd up against narrow streets, with no parking provisions. A fee parking lot next to the beach is the first place a casual visitor can stop and get out of his automobile. More parking lots are south of the first one, handy to the clam beds just inside the bay mouth.

The beach proper occupies a low, rolling plain. Offshore sand bars make swimming safe at the northerly beach. There is ferry service to the offshore sand bars called Sand Island and Long Island where the clams are.

A full line of equipment is available for rent to clammers, crabbers, and fishermen.

## The Sonoma coast

It begins, the Sonoma County coastline, at Bodega Bay, and grows ever more lonely all the way north to the mouth of the Gualala River. It has a bleak beauty about it— not as dramatic as the Big Sur because there are no Santa Lucia Mountains towering up from the water—that is beginning to attract the summer home seekers, who in turn are attracting large-scale land developers. It is going to take a long time to crowd this part of the world.

**Bodega,** the name of a Spanish explorer who passed this way as the No. 2 man in Heceta's expedition, presently describes a town, a headland, and the bay that comes between them. The town serves as headquarters for a sizable fleet of commercial fishermen and charter operators because the bay is the last suitably protected

*Sheep* in the meadows at Marshall

*Clam digging* is rewarding at Dillon Beach

anchorage until Noyo Harbor and because the fishing is good. Sports fishermen and skin divers use the bay extensively, too.

**Doran Beach County Park** is the name of a curving sandspit that reaches across Bodega Bay almost to Bodega Head. It forms an inner and outer harbor for the bay—a natural breakwater—and is also the site of a county launching ramp for small boats (for a small fee) and a favorite takeoff point for skin divers who poke about the marine gardens on the bottom around the bell buoy. The access road heads west from Valley Ford Cut-off road about a mile south of Bodega town.

There is some clamming, mostly for gapers, in the inner harbor from the base of the spit up the eastern shore most of the way to town. The biggest beds are on an offshore bar that uncovers only on low tides.

Bodega Head's fame rests upon the seemingly endless sand dunes that make up its base and much of its length, and upon a large and controversial hole dug in its rocky outer end. The hole was dug to receive a nuclear power plant, to be operated by Pacific Gas & Electric Company. The presence just offshore of the San Andreas Fault gave rise to the controversy. An impasse achieved in 1964 seems likely to endure until one side acquires a crushing weight of evidence or latent support from hitherto silent quarters.

**Salmon Creek State Beach,** the southernmost unit of Sonoma Beaches State Park, attracts considerable numbers of visitors to the ocean side of Bodega Head. Several thousands of California children have romped in great high glee through the sand dunes noted above.

Surfers know the beach well enough and appreciate its merits enough to hold some of their regional competitions on it.

Salmon Creek itself forms a lagoon in summer that affords some wading. In winter, the bar breaks and some salmon and steelhead enter the stream.

Access is from State 1 at the hamlet of Salmon Creek, 1½ miles north of Bodega. A parking area and restrooms are near the highway entry point.

**Arch Rock State Beach** begins just north of the creek and is succeeded by the continuous beaches called **Carnet Beach, Schoolhouse Beach, Portuguese Beach.** They put a sudden end to sand dunes and surfing, replacing these pastimes with abaloning, rock fishing, and tidepool exploring. Going gets fair rocky in places along the shore, but State 1 follows its wrinkly route right behind the beaches. Turnouts are plentiful, and access is always easy.

**Wright Beach** next in the chain, has some of the broadest and sandiest beach front in the park, and it is a picnicker's favorite in addition to being the camping unit of Sonoma State Beaches. There are rocky outcrops for tidepoolers and abaloners.

**Shell Beach** adjoins Wright on the north, a good beach for rockfishing and tidepooling, then it is a solid march to the Russian River through **Blind Beach** and on to **Goat Rock Beach** which terminates of necessity on the south spit of the river mouth, just across from the wee, weathered town of Jenner. Steelheaders line the river shore shoulder to shoulder when the fall run starts across the bar.

All of these beaches face the Pacific head on, a boon to

*Patience is byword for poke-polers*

driftwood collectors, and a menace to any who arrive in ignorance of the strong currents and some of the most unpredictable wave action on the continent.

At Duncan's Point, in the Wright Beach section of the park, a large sign looms up in front of a barbed wire fence. It notes that 21 persons have been swept off the point to their deaths in the pounding sea. None of the bodies was ever recovered, and none had a chance to tell the story, but, presumably, each of the victims felt safe on some perch several feet above the upward rush of the prevailing waves. Obviously, all were in error.

Most occasional beachcombers have heard something of the legend of "every seventh wave" or some such. It has the merest germ of truth in it— that some waves are bigger than others. What happens is simple enough to explain but impossible to predict. Waves are the result of wind pushing against the surface of the water. All the waves originating with one storm tend to be about the same height and evenly spaced apart after they move out of the storm area. These are the swells of the open ocean. However, it is seldom the case that all the waves striking a coast are from just one storm. They are usually the mixed bag that comes of two or three sets of waves intersecting with each other. When different sets of waves start coming together, the regularity of both height and space breaks down. The crest of one wave joining the trough of a wave from the other set cancels both of them out to a considerable degree. But when two crests come together with precision, the resulting single wave begins to be im-

## *Poke-pole fishing*

Sometimes, when an excuse is wanting, a poke-pole expedition for blennies will get a man out of his easy chair and out to the slippery, life-rich rocks in the world between tides.

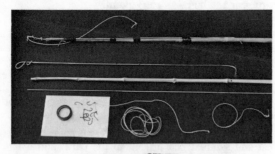

MONKEYFACE EEL (BLENNY-EEL) *Cebidichthys violaceus*

ROCK EEL (ROCK BLENNY) *Xiphister mucosus*

Wherever people angle for rockfish, the blenny is likely to be about. Blenny eel is about as loosely descriptive as the word dog. It covers a whole flock of long slim fish usually but inaccurately known as eels. (The technical consideration is that an eel has to migrate to fresh water to spawn, but these fish look so much like eels they will always be called eels in spite of their failure to live by the code.) The two blennies that concern fishermen are the monkeyface eel (*Cebidichthys violaceus*)and the rock eel (*Xiphister mucosus*). Both grow to a length of 30 inches, and as far as fishermen care their habits are identical.

The blennies spend their lives a few feet under water, in the spacious cavities between big rocks, where the sea surges with each wave even at low tide. The bigger the hole, the bigger the fish are likely to be. They particularly favor areas where sinuous flags of seaweed make a home for the small creatures they seek as food.

Extreme minus tides offer the best fishing, but any low tide is suitable. (The burden is on the fisherman to scout a path that will not leave him trapped by a rising tide, and also to keep a wary eye on abnormally big waves that roll ashore on an erratic schedule.)

Equipment costs little, but has to be assembled by the incipient fisherman. The prime piece is a length of bamboo. Common yellow bamboo is fine. Brown Indian bamboo is better. The length should be determined by the prevailing local distance between a safe perch and the water. Typically, 10 to 12 feet is right. A short pole

pressively larger than its fellows. If still a third wave crest coincides with this large wave, there results the kind of wave that caught the 21 misfortunate souls and swept them off Duncan's Point.

For all of that, there is plenty of safe rock fishing territory in these parks. Skin divers, too, find abaloning and general exploring satisfactory for much of the length of Sonoma State Beaches' 13 miles.

## A RUSSIAN FORT

**Fort Ross** is 13 miles north of Jenner, where State 1 turns toward the sea and begins to dip down from one of the high meadows it crosses for mile after mile. The unmistakably Russian outline of the chapel comes into view first.

This was the center of all Russian fur-trading operations in California from 1812 until the 1840's, and is the last visible remnant of that occupation. The Russians were an extremely commercial lot in those days, at least, and they had in mind decking out (at fancy prices) the world's women in beautiful fur wraps from the lustrous pelt of the sea otter. But, like men before and men since, they got impatient and the women of the world have gone totally without wraps made from sea otter pelts for more than a century. The Russian managers and their Aleut hunters wiped out the sea otter herds to the point of extinction, with minor help from American and British competitors.

The Aleuts, who had learned their trade hunting the

*Fort Ross, a sturdy reminder of days gone by*

---

is six feet, and a long one eighteen. A length of welding rod taped to the pole forms the eye. (Bend the inner end and stick in into a hole drilled in the rod to anchor it.) The business end of the hookup is an 18-inch length of cord and a 2/0 or 3/0 long shank hook. Several of these rigs should be ready ahead of time. A few snag on every trip.

The other essentials for an expedition are a fish knife, a gunny sack, and a rag for blenny-holding and hand-wiping.

Bait is simple. Bought frozen shrimp works if it is broken into small bits. Many veterans pry mussels from the rocks, cut them open at the rounded end of the shell, and cut out the flesh, using the tough muscle to secure the meat on the hook.

The remaining steps are to poke the business end of the pole into the water in a likely looking spot, all the way to the bottom, and to wait. The blenny takes a hook with one sharp tug. Five minutes in one hole without a bite means move along. A hole that yields one fish likely will yield more.

A complication exists in the warm water south of Point Conception. The same technique of fishing may produce a moray or a wolf eel, either of which couples vile temper with sharp teeth and enough jaw muscle to sever a human finger. They should be killed before they are touched. The easy way out is to sacrifice the hook and line.

Even blennies should be dispatched before they are unhooked. Their teeth are no joke either.

Those who weary of fishing for blennies can vary the exercise by angling for greenlings, cabezon, perch, or whatever rockfish will rise to the bait. Extend the pole as far out as balance permits, then let the tip sink slowly toward the bottom. At varying intervals, raise the pole and repeat the maneuver.

Catching blennies requires only moderate concentration. Cooking them should be approached with real precision, or the eater may prejudice himself against blenny flesh for a great long time. The following regimen produces a reasonably delicate flavor.

Wash the fish in cold water, then hang it on a firm support with a nail, or with string tied through the mouth, and skin it.

Use a razor blade, or a very sharp knife. Cut all around the dorsal fin that runs the full length of the body. The cut should be a V-shaped wedge a half inch deep. Then cut around the bottom fin that runs from the middle of the fish to its tail. Do not remove the fins yet.

Cut the skin all the way around the fish just behind its head. Take hold of the skin at this last cut with pliers, and work it down toward the tail, cutting as necessary. The skin should come away in one piece. Holding the fish firmly, grasp the dorsal fin at the tail end with the pliers and pull out and up. Move the pliers forward about an inch at a time, and the entire fin will come out as one piece. Do the same with the bottom fin. Now cut into the body cavity and remove all the entrails.

Fillet the meat. Cook it by simmering the fillets for three minutes in a saucepan of water with two tablespoons of vinegar (the vinegar eliminates the strong fish flavor). Then roll the fillets in egg and crumbs, and fry in butter. When they are nearly done, squeeze lemon juice over them.

*Coast Highway One* and the Pacific Ocean play tag along the scenic Mendocino coast

Alaska herds of the same animal, were deadly efficient. Working from two man kayaks, they hunted in fleets. Several of the canoes would form a circle, then start constricting the perimeter. When the animals surfaced to breathe, they were harpooned. The carcasses were retrieved by means of lines attached to the harpoons, which were then thrown again. When things got slow, the hunters would take a pup alive and use its distress cries to lure adults into range.

A museum in the old commandant's quarters tells the essential story with paraphernalia left behind after the hunters had succeeded all too well. It is both a state park and national monument.

Below the fort, picnic tables ring a small sandy beach at the mouth of Fort Ross Creek. Rocky headlands close the beach off north and south, and the area is popular with skin divers, most of them hunting abalones.

North beyond the fort there is only one more park with beach front along the Sonoma County coast.

Salt Point State Beach is one of the pioneer units in California's marine park system, a new approach which will put the underwater side of the shore within reach of park users. It remains for the park to be developed along these lines. Meantime it is a good conventional beach, especially for tidepoolers.

Salt Point is just south of Kruse Rhododendron Reserve, about midway between Jenner and Stewarts Point.

A dirt road forks northwest off State 1 without any fanfare, and follows a sketchy fence across meadows that top a lofty bluff. From the parking area, one path leads steeply down to a cove. By bearing a few hundred yards west and north across sloping meadow, visitors come down to a rock-strewn shore which runs a lumpy but uninterrupted mile north.

Otherwise, this part of the coast is getting private development. Sea Ranch is the biggest property of the lot, four miles north of the Stewarts Point Road junction. Timber Cove, which also has an inn, is a mile north of Fort Ross.

## Mendocino's coast

Mendocino's coast, mostly steep bluffs and craggy headlands separated by rocky little beaches, sets people who know some to whistling Cornish folk airs.

There is something of Cornwall about the place. There are sheep in the meadows (and the road). The weather glooms a great deal, but has fits of brightness in spring and fall that astound even the pioneers with the beauty of the scene. Of the forests that led to Mendocino's settlement in the first place, there are left a few fine stands of fir that comes all the way down to the shore, and a great

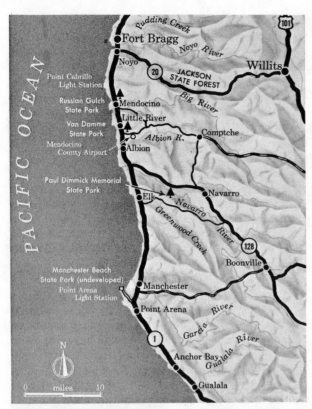

SHORESIDE CAMPING: Van Damme State Park (82 units); Russian Gulch State Park (35 units); MacKerricher State Park (156 units). SHORESIDE ACCOMMODA-TIONS: Main concentrations at Fort Bragg-Noyo, Mendocino town. Sprinkling of motels, inns all along highway. No list.

Rock fishermen throw out a line and wait

many more that march along the ridges a mile or so back from the sea and 200 feet above it.

The coast highway goes along a high meadow, turns east and dips down to a creek bed, across, turns sharply west and climbs the far bank to another meadow, and then begins the process again for the nth time. It keeps on doing that for 100 miles without wearing out the idea.

Unhappily, there is no Cornish Coastal Footpath here as there is in the original Cornwall, going the whole distance. At least the state parks have a few hiking trails that go along in unspoiled and uncrowded grasslands above the sea.

Skin divers and rock fishermen get great mileage out of the relatively small amount of publicly accessible shore.

**Gualala** just across the Gualala River from Sonoma County, and Manchester 22 miles north, are the outposts of a small population belt centering on Point Arena. Gualala for its part was and is a small lumber and mill town perched just at the river mouth, while Manchester is a farm community set in the middle of an extensive coastal plain. Between the two are Anchor Bay, whose beaches have latterly starred in a movie, and Point Arena, which has a charming town and a photogenic lighthouse on its flanks.

The course of the Gualala River parallel to the coast-line is, incidentally, another manifestation of the San Andreas Fault.

**Anchor Bay's** few houses look out to sea from a pine-covered terrace. Below the terrace is a rocky stretch of shore that has a privately-owned campground with beach access.

It was in this area that a motion picture called "Island of the Blue Dolphins" was made in the fall of 1963. The story is a true one of the unhappy accidents befalling a young local Indian maiden upon the arrival of some marauding Aleut hunters (the poor Aleuts just do not come off as nice guys in California history). It passed through the nation's theaters with high critical acclaim but without exciting much interest at the box office. No fault can be laid at the door of the Mendocino coast, which turned its sunniest face to the cameras.

Rockhounds occasionally turn up a fossil seashell at the Anchor Bay beach.

**Point Arena** might have been a major salmon fishing port were it not for the infrequent storm out of the south-west. The small harbor exposes itself completely to that quarter, and there is nothing to be done about it. So, the enormous anchor ring lies little used on the town beach, a source of wonderment to the landbound tourists who encounter it by chance.

North of town, Lighthouse Road heads west, predict-ably, to Point Arena Light, the most powerful on this coast. The wave-swept headland is a dramatic one, even by exacting local standards.

*The rocky Mendocino coast takes a rest at Anchor Bay—one of the area's few sandy beaches*

**Manchester Beach State Park,** within hailing distance to the north of the light, but inaccessible from that direction because of wide-mouthed Garcia River, does not yet have any improvements to show for its status. A road leads from State 1 down to the beach. The turnoff, marked by a small sign, is about 3 miles north of town. This beach is broad and sandy (and attractive to smelt), one of the few such in this south part of the county coast, and heavily littered with driftwood. Rocky outcrops of uptilted sedimentary stone begin at the south edge of the park and extend all the way back to the town. In these rocks are some of the least trammeled tidepools of the California coastline. The range of intertidal animals is, further, complete for prevailing conditions.

**Alder Creek,** a mile and a half north of Manchester, terminates a stretch of seven sandy miles that has its other end at Manchester Beach. A spur road leads down close to the creek mouth, where salmon and steelhead fishermen find the waters productive in spawning season. This is good driftwood hunting and beachcombing country. The Mendocino Coast has a century-long history of coastwise shipping, and there was a sizable Indian population here before the lumbermen came in the 1840s. Both the Indians and the seafarers left bits and pieces of the wreckage within reach of the tides and waves. Astute hunters can still turn

up a timber from an old steam schooner, or a battered piece of what once was a canoe.

**Albion** with its high graceful bridge soaring over a tiny, three-boat harbor, marks the beginning of that section of Mendocino Coast that most visitors think of as the real thing. From here to Mendocino town, old inns, restaurants, motels, and some of California's best artists attract the roving curiosity of tourists who come out from San Francisco and other urban centers to envy the quiet solitude this coast offers.

North and south of Albion, the inns and motels frequently control access to the beaches. Guests at these places can get down to tiny coves, or out onto miniature low-tide islands not accessible to motorists passing through.

If there seems to be a general absence of interesting drift on the accessible beaches in these parts, it is because professionals work the shore here every day, with a knowledge born of long experience with local tides and currents, and a strong motivation to get up at some unsaintly hour like 3 a.m. to follow the high tide in and out.

The resort guest can hope to find something of use, especially in the off season.

Beach photographers have better odds going for them.

The multitude of fast (in winter) creeks along this coast, coupled with the amount of logging that goes on, means an abundance of worn old stumps and roots everywhere along the shore. With their backdrops of offshore rocks, wave-tunneled islets, and grassy headlands with one or two wind-bent pines at the tip, these offer endless opportunities for striking compositions, abstracts, and texture studies. And those stumps are too big for anybody to cart away very easily.

**Van Damme State Park** comes down to the shore in a small cove at Little River. An Englishman looking underfoot would say that this was a genuine shingle, because the fist-sized and smaller stones underfoot look very much like the ones on the English beaches where the word was coined. At the north side of the cove, outthrust rocks close off exploration in a short distance beyond the parking lot that occupies the narrow space between the beach and State 1. To the south, it is possible to walk a little more than a quarter of a mile before rocks bar further passage.

A few fire rings and picnic tables are set to give passers-by a pleasant view out to the reef of rocks that calm the water inside the bay so lifetime cardholders in polar bear clubs can swim free of currents and heavy surf in 52° water.

The beach is a pleasant wayside stop, but is only a minor introduction to the park, which is more oriented toward the thick stands of pines, the spacious meadows, and the fern-filled creek canyon on the inland side of the highway. Deer abound in the park, where they are chased by small boys and sheep, but not enough to drive them away.

Occasionally a daring sailboater will come to anchor in the small bay, which is better protected than Mendocino Bay, to arouse great envy among car-bound tourists in the area. Sometimes these romantically mysterious visitors from the sea get a comeuppance when the surf mounts unexpectedly and gets so turbulent around the reef that the sailor has to wait it out, pitching and rolling heavily while the motorist smiles from solid ground.

**Mendocino** town, an anachronistic collection of wooden water towers and carpenter's gothic which houses a fully contemporary society of long-time residents and newly come artists, faces two ways—south across its deep-sided bay and west across wave-sculpted bluffs to the open ocean.

Rock fishermen come in numbers to the old lumber-loading chute next to the garbage dump at the west end of Main street. It requires some scrambling down the rocks to get to favored perches (which is an accurate pun on the probable catch), but the effort usually has tangible rewards.

Around the point from this bay-facing outlook is a wide grassy bluff with more than a mile of shoreline. A loop road extending west from the downtown platte runs along the edges of the bluff. Turnouts and parking places are ample in size and number.

The area is called Heeser Drive after newspaper publisher August Heeser, who made it accessible to the public as a gift to the town. It is a highly sculpted shore, with wave tunnels, arched rocks, narrow channels, and even a few lagoon-like bodies. The tidepooling is fine. Skin divers do well at anything they care to pursue. The easiest and most pleasant activity, though, is scrambling

around the rocks to watch an unusually picturesque surf pound its way through the jumble of rocks, with the strong possibility of having a harbor seal or sea lion watching back, seemingly unconcerned by the surf's violence.

After some hours of watching out to the horizon and underfoot, it is instructive to go back to town to see how some of the resident artists—Dorr Bothwell, Kent Bowman, Emmy Lou Packard, Hilda Pertha and Byron Randall are among them—look upon this shore. Emmy Lou Packard in particular expends much of her creative energy on prints and paintings of the sea, and especially tidepool animals. (She maintains some saltwater aquaria in her gallery to have subjects ready at hand.)

**Russian Gulch State Park** a bit more than two miles north of Mendocino town, with access from State 1, offers the inveterate beachcomber a good deal more room to roam than does Van Damme. The creek cuts out of the gulch, across a sandy low spot that provides wading and splashing pools for children, then slips into the sea in the lee of a particularly craggy point of rock. This latter point is sometimes called the north coast counterpart of Point Lobos. Like its supposed relation, it has a multitude of trails leading to deep coves, and out onto rocks where intertidal life teems in large and small pools of water trapped when the tide goes out. The fishing from these rocks has produced good catches for several generations of anglers. Abaloning is good for divers. It is a fine camping park, with most of its sites on the bluffs.

**Point Cabrillo Light** a mile north of the park and a mile west of State 1 on a coast guard road commands a remarkable view of the quality of this coast that reminds some people of Cornwall. On an autumn day when the fog retreats offshore, a visitor can peer northward for miles, with the blue sea, the white surf, and the grassy brown bluffs sharply etched against the sky. The lighthouse itself is probably doomed to fall into the sea at some distant day. The present occupants needn't worry, but the whole headland on which the light sits is riddled with wave tunnels, some of which end inland from the light itself. The effect is both unnerving and rare to see.

State 1 loops inland a bit north of the light, and stays up in the meadows all the way to Noyo Harbor at the south side of Fort Bragg, the commercial center for the whole coastal plain in Mendocino County. The enormous Pacific Union Lumber Company controls the shore in town, although it can be idly pleasant wandering along the jetty at Noyo.

**MacKerricher Beach State Park** four miles north of town is sandy after all that rock to the south. It's not all sandy. The park has rocks where the fishing, tidepooling, and abalone diving are good. But the main beach is black sand and battered by a heavy surf that comes rushing up the steep beach face all full of smelt in season.

North, the sand dunes roll on and on, on what is called Ten Mile Beach. The land belongs to the lumber company, but is accessible along the tideline if not by road.

**Westport Union Landing Beach State Park** 17 miles north of Fort Bragg, is hard to say and lacks for dramatic scenery, but it is another fine beach for smelt fishermen. It is the most northerly park in Mendocino County. It is flanked north and south by undeveloped lands which permit beach access to the persistent.

# The redwood coast

The far north coast of California is famous for one commodity, *Sequoia sempervirens*, or the Coast Redwood. These matchless and ageless trees are at root the entirety of the regional economy.

Most of them are logged to make fine lumber, or souvenir trinkets, depending on which part of the tree is under manufacture. A few sizable preserves are retained for visitors to look up into with awe, and as such are the cause of a sizable tourist industry. Eureka is a commercial fishing port of some size, but the gross income from this industry is far, far behind the revenue produced by the forests.

The terrain from the general vicinity of Eureka north

**SHORESIDE CAMPING:** *None.* **SHORESIDE ACCOMMODATIONS:** *Crescent City on highway south of central district, and west of highway in central district; Smith River has many.*

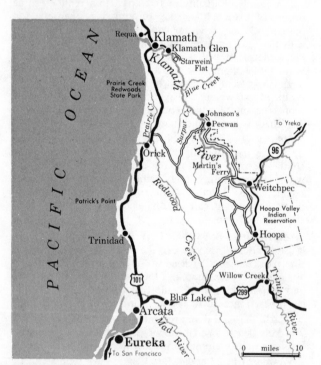

**SHORESIDE CAMPING:** *Patricks Point State Park (6 mi. no. of Trinidad) (122 units); Prairie Creek Redwoods State Park (7 mi. no. of Orick) (100 units).* **SHORESIDE ACCOMMODATIONS:** *Very few. Eureka has many motels inshore. A few motels are on U.S. 101 north of Trinidad, also well inshore.*

to the California-Oregon border is rugged. Forested hills crowd against the ocean shore most of the distance. The rather limited amount of beach open to easy exploration is attractive, however, to smelters, clammers, surf and rock fishermen, driftwood hunters, and rockhounds. Salmon fishermen of every persuasion from deep sea to river bank flock to the area, and in fact are the prime fall users of shoreside accommodations all along the coast.

**Redwood National Park**, made up of three great state parks, is mostly in the lee of the first rank of coastal hills to profit from improvement in the inshore weather. The shore has some of the cloudiest, rainiest climate in California. Eureka, for example, wins the "coolest city in the nation" title almost daily in summer. But such dampness is no reason to stay away from the seaside parks in this region, gratuitous advice to the crowds that use them.

# Around Eureka

The venerable fishing and lumbering capital of northern California's redwood country sits on a minor knoll or two between the oft-flooded plains of the Mad and Van Duzen Rivers, and on the highly industrialized shore of Humboldt Bay. Its waterfront is as grimy as mill town water fronts always are, but the rest of the town and the country around it are pleasant throwbacks to an earlier, less speedy time in California.

This is a spacious part of the world, and Humboldt is a good sized bay. Heading north or south out of Eureka means just that to the recreation-minded. There is no going both ways in one day.

South, the shore is very difficult to reach with the exceptions of the bay's south spit and two parks just south of the base of the spit. The difficulty owes to the almost complete lack of roads in the massive protrusion that is Cape Mendocino. North there is more shore attended by more people. The Redwood Highway, busy all summer, runs close to the edge of the sea for a very great part of the distance to the county line.

### SOUTH OF EUREKA

Once past the sportfishing pier south of town (Fields Landing), U. S. 101 begins to bend away from the shore for its long and justly famous excursion through the groves of redwood trees (the big ones that most visitors recall to mind after they are home and showing slides).

Just south of the bay, at Beatrice, a two-lane road turns west off the highway and pursues its course to the ocean shore near Table Bluff Light, which occupies that bluff rising up from the base of the bay spit. The light looks out over a series of huge underwater sandbars that help to create some of the wildest winter surf open to view on this coast.

The surf is not good for much of anything but watching. Swimming is out of the question because of the waves and strong currents. The waves are not the right kind for surfing. The area is more than a hundred miles too far

*New **addition** to Prairie Creek Redwoods State Park—the long, inviting strand of Gold Beach*

north for Pismo clams, and it is at the southern extreme of the range of razor clams. (There are some on the spit, but the bigger local beds are north of Samoa.)

For wave watching, though, it is very good. During the war a team of scientists was engaged in surveying the underwater topography of this coast in the interests of seeing how the bed of the sea affects waves. The immediate purpose was to improve site selection for amphibious invasions. Their technique was to make soundings from a Duck as it hurtled ashore, an immense, motorized surfboard.

Soon after they started the Coast Guard crewmen at the Table Bluff lifesaving station paid a call to tell the scientists to stop, or to absolve the Coast Guard of any responsibility for their safety. The scientists, being under contract to the U.S. Navy, could not stop, and at all events were loathe to call a halt to a highly exciting duty toward the war effort.

One of their number, Willard Bascom, wrote a book on the general subject of waves and beaches, appropriately entitled *Waves and Beaches* (Dover, $1.95), and in it are some anecdotes about the adventures along with a wealth of good information on the main subject.

The Coast Guard attitude sums up what needs to be said about the rough seas there.

There is another, more workaday hazard to visiting the area. The road out the south spit is long, flat, and straight. It is much used by apprentice auto drivers.

**Clam Park** is the name of the undeveloped county park near the lighthouse. It is a popular picnicking spot with clammers and surf fishermen, and with drift hunters.

**Centerville Beach County Park** is a few miles downshore on the other side of the Mad River, and reached by a different route, west off U.S. 101 at the turn off for Ferndale, through Ferndale, and on to the shore on a plainly marked county road. The entertainments are much like those at Clam Park, but in more developed surroundings. The park has water, restrooms, and picnic tables. Local driftwood collectors visit this park and the shore accessible from it as regularly as any place in the immediate region. The park is 24 miles from downtown Eureka, the roads good all the way.

## THE UNKNOWN COAST

The Unknown Coast, which is getting better known with each passing day, is the longest roadless section of the United States' Pacific shoreline, not counting Alaska. It reaches 40 miles from Cape Mendocino south to a point beyond Shelter Cove, where California Highway 1 turns inland to connect with U.S. 101. Most of the area is still under blanketing forest, most of it redwood. Its main use has been as a low-intensity ranching and farming area. Because of that, it is crossed by a sketchy, even impromptu set of roads and wagon tracks.

Shelter Cove is the reason it is getting better known. The rugged beauty of the area captivated a development corporation, which began in 1964 to open the shore to vacation home seekers. The immediate area is now possessed of an air field, a street grid, and is scheduled to gain a golf course and other civilizing marks.

At all events, the gravel road from Garberville on U.S. 101 to Shelter Cove is now being maintained in good condition for modern automobiles. The rest of the roads in the region are not adapted to any low-slung automobile.

*On a stormy coast* Trinidad Light warns ships against rocky shore below

Four wheel drive cars are the only bet for anybody who wants to take a north-south tour on the Honeydew-Petrolia-Capetown road in company of an occasional logging truck. For a dedicated byway explorer, this is one place to spend a few days going one up on some of the fellow-types.

There are a couple of aged lodges at Mattole, mainly used by hunters, and the King Range National Conservation Area has four small campgrounds in it, with a total of 34 family camping sites. (These are Nadelos, on King Range Road two miles south of Shelter Cove Road, 22 miles west of U.S. 101; Wailaki, one mile due west of Nadelos; Tolkan, four miles north of Shelter Cove Road and 24 miles west of U.S. 101; and Horse Mountain, six miles north of Shelter Cove Road and 26 miles west of the main highway.) Each campground provides access to the shore by way of trails.

It is not worth going in deer season, except for deer hunters.

## NORTH OF EUREKA

The north loop of Humboldt Bay is cupped in low-lying ground, the shoreward edge of which has episodic merit as a clamming grounds, and fairly consistent merit as a place for surf fishing. It does not, for some miles, have the kind of elevations that provide good scenery.

**Samoa** is a mill town on the north spit of the bay, which is reached by way of a county road that exits from U.S. 101 at Arcata. The presence of industrial mills on the spit does little to enhance its scenic worth, and keeps the bay side waters little usable by beach-oriented folk. But the ocean shore remains relatively clean, and it yields clams, surf fish, and occasional driftwood pieces.

**Mad River County Park** at the mouth of the river of the same name, and accessible from U.S. 101 on a river bank road, is 16 miles from Eureka, which supplies the greater number of the surf fishermen, beach hikers, driftwood hunters, and picnickers who come to it in good weather and bad. The only facility is parking.

**Little River State Park** and **Clam Beach County Park** are also 16 miles north of Eureka, but in a straight line on the highway. The road returns to the shore at the point of the parks after ambling along inland north of Arcata. The road runs right along the back shore just a few yards from the sand. There are no turnouts, however. Only two exits from the highway permit access to a frontage road and the park parking lots. One of these is open only to southbound traffic, and is marked Clam Beach. The other is good in either direction, and it is the signed exit for the village of Crannell. The two parks adjoin each other and are wholly indistinguishable to anybody except maybe a surveyor. Both are broad strands backed by the fence that separates them from the highway, and fronted by a shoaling beach with clams in it.

The clam that gives the park its name is the razor, here at the southern limit of its range. By Washington or Oregon standards, it is not numerous, but a skilled digger will find a few, especially during a good minus tide in the dead of winter when the competition is not so fierce.

## TRINIDAD AND NORTH

Very shortly north of Little River and the parks noted above, the rocky nature that dominates the California coast all the way to Oregon's border begins to assert itself. The results are picturesque both from the highway and from closer to the water's edge.

Trinidad is the name of a small fishing town that is also the most northerly commute town in the state. The fishing harbor is a small one. The commuters are some of Eureka's professional people who are willing to hurtle back and forth on the freeway in return for the fine scenery and pleasant homes of the town.

One pleasant part of the scenery is the lighthouse, poised on the shoulder of a roundish hill that barely qualifies as a part of the mainland. The functioning light is not to be confused with the old one, which, without its lamp, sits alongside the street high above the harbor shore as a memorial to fishermen lost at sea. Visitors exiting from the highway can drive straight west to the memorial light. From there, the big hill that forms the hook of the harbor is in easy view. The operating light is on the west side of it, and the road goes right on to it.

Where the road dips down onto a low-lying, skinny neck of sand, fishermen turn left to the fishing harbor while lighthouse buffs keep straight and go up the hill. Visiting hours are 1 to 4 p.m. weekends.

The small fishing harbor is mainly commercial, but there is a party boat for sports fishermen, who do well in these waters, which have a fair share of salmon.

**Trinidad Beach State Park** is in the northwest quarter of the town, at the foot of the hill below the school. Motorists should bear north from the freeway exit to get to the school. The park entrance is just west of it. One of the park's prime allures is good surf fishing, and it is a favored picnicking place. A strong running surf and cold water rule it out as a swimming beach, and there are better places for skin divers, even though the department of marine biology of Humboldt State College (of Arcata) is building a laboratory in the town.

**Luffenholtz County Park** is one of those "better places" for skin divers and tidepoolers. It is two miles south of Trinidad, at a point where the offshore waters are full of seastacks and less definable rocks. It makes for fine wave watching, too, and the surf fishing is good. The beach is sandy enough for some pleasant walking on the way to tidepools, or in quest of wood or other drift.

## The ocean in motion — Tides

Tides, waves, and currents keep matters in a constant state of flux wherever the ocean comes ashore. Between them, these forces move millions of tons of sand around, pitch boulders through the roofs of lighthouses, create good living conditions for Pismo clams in one place and keyhole limpets in another, and please or aggravate human beings whose attitudes toward the sea are heavily dependent upon highway driving times, school hours, and the price of clams in restaurants.

An apprentice user of the shore does well to learn a few facts about the workings of the ocean in motion. They improve his chances of catching something whilst avoiding being caught.

The tides are in effect twice-daily waves that sweep like the hour hand of a clock about an axis point in mid-ocean. The crests of the two waves are high tides, and the troughs low tides.

These waves, running 12 hours and 25 minutes apart, are the product of an otherwise insignificant disequilibrium among the sun, the moon, and the earth. Their local nature owes to underwater topography, which produces some showy variations in a generally undramatic global scheme.

The moon, circling at an average distance of 239,000 miles, pulls at the surface of the earth nearest it. Rock barely responds, but the ocean humps up liquidly. On the opposite side of the world a similar bump of water occurs because the opposing centrifugal force of the earth curving through its orbit comes close to matching the pull of the moon.

The effect of the sun is a different one. It exerts a very slight pull, but one that is almost equal on each side of the earth. It tugs across 93 million miles of space, and the 4,000 mile thickness of the earth is irrelevant. Its contribution is to reinforce the effect of the moon when the two bodies are aligned relative to the earth (producing the extreme high and low tides called spring tides), and to counter the effect of the moon when the two pull at right angles to each other (producing the minimum variations called neap tides). Spring tides occur at new moon and full moon, neaps at the quarters.

Another effect is produced by the irregularity of the moon's orbit around the earth. When it comes closest, extreme tides result because of this. At least twice a year the moon is close to the earth at the same time it aligns with the sun. On these days clam diggers get at beds they can't touch at any other time.

In the open ocean tides hardly matter. On some mid-Pacific islands, only an expert knows whether it is high tide or low. It is the continental shelf, functioning like a wedge beneath the oncoming wave, that produces the kind of tides a man notices.

The exact nature of shore topography determines finally how the local tide works. On the sandy stretches of Washington and Oregon where the underwater slope is gradual, water retreats and advances long distances. On the rocky coasts, where bluffs drop into deep water, the only thing exposed by a low tide is an extra band of rock. Bays with narrow mouths produce strong currents on ebbing tides, especially if they are also fed by rivers.

If the entire coast were straight as a ruler, with a smooth offshore shelf, the tides would advance along it at a constant speed. But the coast is all knobby, and tides progress at a rather less even rate.

Computers can predict tides, and they do. The results are published in an annual book of tide tables by the U.S. Coast and Geodetic Survey. The listed stations for the U.S. coast are San Diego, Los Angeles (outer harbor), San Francisco, Humboldt Bay, Astoria (Ore.), Aberdeen, and Port Townsend. A supplementary table gives instructions for correcting times and tides for a number of intermediate points.

To give some idea of how a tide progresses, the following is a sketchy history of the lower low tide of September 19-20, 1965: San Diego, 11:43 p.m. (—0.2); Los Angeles, 11:36 p.m. (0.0); San Francisco, 1:12 a.m. (—0.3); Humboldt Bay, 1:45 a.m. (—0.1); Newport, Ore., 2:45 a.m. (0.0); Astoria, 3:09 a.m. (—0.4); Copalis Beach, Wash., 3:49 a.m. (—0.1), and Port Townsend, 5:06 a.m. (—0.9).

# The ocean in motion — Waves

Waves are not water on the way somewhere else. They are, as much as anything, potential energy travelling in a visible form. The distance a good wave can travel ranges upward of 5,000 miles. In fact, some of the waves that approach the California coast from the south are at the end of a trip begun in a storm off New Zealand.

Waves begin, innocently enough, when a freshening sea wind blowing across the surface causes ripples to form as a result of friction. Once a ripple forms, its windward side traps wind force ever more efficiently and it continues to grow. The effect in a storm area is often confused, but the force of a storm has a general direction. Once the waves outrun the wind this becomes evident as they settle into the regular height and spacing of open ocean swells, the kind that make stomachs uneasy aboard passenger ships.

Nothing much happens until the column of energy stored in the wave touches bottom in shallow water. Then the potential energy of the swell turns into the real energy of surf.

A wave breaks when the ratio of wave height to water depth reaches 4:3. Depending on the nature of the bottom, this can happen slowly and gently, or quickly and violently. The original height of the wave determines how far offshore the surf zone starts during any one prevailing condition.

As a wave reaches shallow water, its front edge slows down sooner than the back side. This causes its column of energy to compress. The wave gets both thinner and taller until it becomes unstable and falls.

A gently shoaling beach does not produce crashing surf. It deprives the wave of a considerable amount of its energy with bottom friction increased so slowly that the wave remains stable—the spilling breaker that surfers ride—most of the way to the shore. By then its force is largely spent. This is especially true where the bottom is also irregular with rocks or holes.

Wide surf zones have a series of sand bars and troughs that have big breakers on the outer bar, and smaller ones on each succeeding bar inside.

If the approach to the outer bar is steep, plunging breakers result. Succeeding waves are smaller and usually a mixture of plunging and spilling breakers.

A very steep approach to a beach means the wave is not affected until the last few moments of its life, when it suddenly towers up and crashes onto the beach face, a perfect plunging breaker of almost frightening violence.

It is possible to get a general picture of the underwater topography of a beach just by studying the way the surf looks. Green water is deep. White water is shallow. Spilling breakers mean gentle slope. Plunging breakers mean steep slope. Three or four lines of breakers mean a series of parallel sand bars with intervening troughs. If a narrow band of green (deep) water extends out through the line of breakers, it means a channel that most probably is returning water from the beach to the sea, or, in short, a rip current.

(A side note—waves meet the shore head on because of the same factors that make them break. If the original approach is at an angle, the end that hits shallow water first slows down a bit, and the whole wave pivots on that end as it rushes the shore.)

*Driftwood hunters*, rockhounds enjoy Pebble Beach

The park is not accessible from the main highway, except through Trinidad. The freeway exit there leads to a blinker light intersection. The road to this park leads south out of that intersection, parallel to the highway for the first few hundred yards.

**Patricks Point State Park,** 27½ miles north of Eureka and fewer than seven miles north of Trinidad, is serendipity. In the midst of the redwood parks, this one is wooded and cool, with meadows scattered through it, and both rocky and sandy beach as its shore. But it is not a redwood park. The few redwoods in it are too scattered out to be its raison d'etre.

The southerly end is the rocky part of the shore, a favored haunt of tidepoolers and rock fishermen. The hills are steep and irregular and laced with formal and informal paths that offer every possibility to adventurous youngsters, and some fairly strenuous strolls to their elders out to take in the scenery. Some of the steepest of the trails follow writhing courses to the tops of tall knolls while others drop sharply to the edge of the sea.

The more northerly half of the shore is a broad strand at the foot of a steep and lofty bluff. This part is known as Agate Beach, and is reached by rockhounds and others only after a rapid descent of a switchback trail down the bluff. It is safe and wide, but a taxing exertion coming and going.

The rest of the park is equally diverting in less salty ways, and has especially pleasant campsites. In early fall the temperature sometimes gets into the mid 70's, when the park fills with campers early in the day.

**Dry Lagoon Beach State Park** and **Big Lagoon County Park** occupy a lowland immediately to the north of Patricks Point, and provide warm swimming in fresh water on one side, and cold fishing in salt water on the other. The area is notably popular with local residents, who also use the lagoons for trout fishing and small boating.

It is possible, if tedious, to walk the shore more than a mile back to the bluff trail in Patricks Point.

The picnic areas are fine. The state park has rather more fully developed bathing facilities than its adjacent county

*Museum* takes up first floor of Crescent City light. It can be approached only at low tide

counterpart. A concessionaire operates in the neighborhood, but Trinidad has the closest full-fledged store.

**Redwood Creek County Park** flanks the lagoons on the north, and its sandy strand is the northerly extreme of the agate beach that begins in Patricks Point State Park. Surf fishing is good along this shore, and it is a good place to hunt drift in winter. There are no developed facilities.

## PRAIRIE CREEK REDWOODS

In late 1965, Gold Beach was added to the official area of Prairie Creek Redwoods, now a part of the national park. While primarily intended to allow a wondering citizenry ample views of the great redwood trees, the park in Gold Beach offers a long expanse of attractive ocean shore as well. Human visitors to this quarter of Prairie Creek's 13,000 acres may need to share space with a roving band of elk; the animals prefer seaside meadow to deep forest.

The shore is broad and sandy, mainly coursing along below steep bluffs. Rocky spots have good tidepools. The sandy stretches, cut here and there by creeks, offer surf fishing, driftwood hunting, and easy beach walking. The shore has been preserved in its primitive state for the most part. The easy way to get to it is along one of several fine hiking trails.

The out-thrusting headlands come within range of high tides. While it is impossible to become dangerously trapped by an incoming tide, it is possible to get trapped into taking the long way back to the campgrounds, or headquarters parking areas. A tide table is, thereby, a useful thing to have along.

Prairie Creek's main entrance is on U.S. 101 north of Eureka 49 miles.

# Del Norte County

Del Norte means "of the north" and it is literal in this instance, Del Norte County being the most northerly one California has.

**Black Sand** at Bear Harbor near Shelter Cove

It is a sparsely populated place, Crescent City being the only incorporated municipality within its boundaries. Fishing and lumbering are its commercial mainstays.

## CRESCENT CITY AND NORTH

Crescent City lends truth to its name. It curves with the broad arc of Crescent Bay. The most attractive parts of the curve tend to lie west of the highway, which passes only through roadside commercial establishments on its way through town.

From the breakwater north, the shore of the town is both scenic and useful to a variety of activists.

**Battery Point Lighthouse** sits on a hummocky, high tide island near the base of the breakwater. The old lighthouse is a museum now, its main floor filled with memorabilia of this and other lighthouses, and an assortment of documents of local maritime history, which is considerable.

The keeper shoos visitors away in time to keep them from being caught by an incoming tide, an event which ordinarily occurs rather sooner than a browser would like.

Just across 'A' Street from the lighthouse is the manufacturing plant for the tetrapods that make up the breakwater for the harbor. Tetrapods are scientifically designed four-footed masses of concrete molded along the lines of ordinary playing jacks. Their shapes are calculated to take the maximum energy out of approaching waves, and Crescent City was the first place in the U.S. to use them. The invention is a French one. A single example of a tetrapod is mounted as a memorial on the highway at the south edge of the city.

North of the light, the shore is rocky and sandy in alternate stretches. A road (A Street, then W. 5th) hugs the crest of the bluff for several blocks, giving regular access to the shore, which is called Pebble Beach because it has much of interest to rockhounds among its stones. There is a good litter of driftwood near the lighthouse, and another one farther north.

Parkouts make it easy to stop at any of several points along the way.

North of the city, county roads give less regular access to similar beaches for most of the distance to the mouth of the Smith River. This is popular clamming territory among local residents, but it takes a few trial runs or a local acquaintance to locate the most promising beds in an unmarked shore.

**Smith River** is famous as a fishing spot. Salmon entering the Smith River to spawn are a major run, and they produce a major run of fishermen. The technique here is to anchor in skiffs at one of three rows just at the mouth of the river, and horse 'em in.

**Pelican Beach State Park,** just north of the river mouth, is a favorite retreat for non-fishermen on fishing expeditions. Tangles of driftwood litter its shore, and some minor sand dunes seem to please youngsters. There are no facilities in the park, but the commercial street of Smith River is in easy walking distance.

## SOUTH OF CRESCENT CITY

Most of the coastline south of Crescent City is abrupt cliffs once south of Crescent Beach. Getting to the edge of the water is a seldom thing, but the panoramic scenery is worth the price.

*Crescent Beach* is south of the main business area of Crescent City. There is a public fishing wharf planted in the middle of the long, low strand. Otherwise it is just long, low, and grassy beach.

Rockhounds patrol some of its gravelly patches. Driftwood hunters cart off immense quantities of that commodity. But the greatest users, in terms of numbers, are the most northerly of California's teen-aged surfboard riders. Usually the waves are less than four feet high, but on the right day they get up toward six feet while remaining properly suited to the riders' purposes.

**Wilson Creek Bridge,** 8 miles north of Klamath, has at its south end a small but pleasantly developed picnic area and walking beach, the only part of Del Norte Redwoods Park developed for easy use by motorists on the way through.

South of it, the tiny sport fishing resorts of Klamath and Requa, west of the highway on the banks of the Klamath River, are the last settlements before Humboldt County. The road between Wilson Creek and the Klamath River edges along the bluffs high above the sea. When the weather is right, it is a fine introduction to California for visitors from the north.

---

## The ocean in motion — Currents

Great currents sweep across the oceans and produce great works, but they do not make an appreciable dent on any one beach. That is left to a whole series of smaller, more fleeting movements of water. Tides cause currents on shallow shelves, between headlands, and around bay mouths. Waves and surf transport a certain amount of water onto the beach, which has to retreat to the sea somehow. Eddies and backwashes from the great oceanic currents play a role, too.

Tidal currents run northward along this coast because the tide progresses in that direction. This general condition is reinforced north of Point Conception by the fact that prevailing winds blow out of the southwest, setting up waves that run northward along the shore. Water piled up in a surf zone will tend to continue in the direction of the waves. But any cove, inlet, or headland will impose its stamp on general currents, and may create a fairly stout counter current as an eddy to some other current.

Watching the progress of drift on the water will demonstrate the direction and speed of the current. Looking closely at the degree of coarseness of sand on a curving beach will provide some clues. The finer the sand, the weaker the current. Also, small drift at one end of a beach and large drift at the other indicates stronger currents where the big stuff comes to rest. (Small particles will remain suspended in a weak current; heavier ones precipitate sooner.)

Almost all sand spits on coast harbors point north, mainly a matter of the tides' sweep.

# OREGON COAST

# Coos Bay to the border

In the southwest corner of Oregon the topography is so rumpled that roads are hardly feasible. In fact, the only major road south of Bandon to the border is the coast highway, U.S. 101. All spur roads in that region dwindle to nothing after only a few miles. A forked route from Roseburg to either Coos Bay or Bandon is the only connection with Interstate 5 and the interior.

A thin thread of civilization clings to the steep flanks of the countless major hills and minor mountains that crowd the shore for most of the distance. The major economic function of these inhabitants is lumber, which industry has its principal center at Coos Bay. Fishing is a distant second, and third place belongs to tourism.

Except at Coos Bay, the basic economy hardly shows its face to the visitor passing through. The ocean views tend to hold his attention, and they are remarkable ones. Panoramas are the main attraction beyond doubt. But for the man with time it is possible to get active about smelting, clamming, crabbing, shore and boat fishing, rockhounding, tidepooling, or drift hunting at a number of points along the way.

Some of the favorite haunts of activists are not obvious

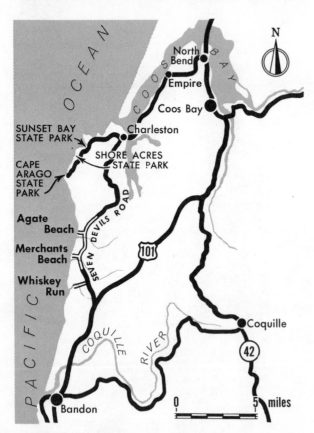

**SHORESIDE CAMPING:** *Sunset Bay State Park (108 units, 29 trailer units); Bastendorff Park (35 units, 30 trailer units).* **SHORESIDE ACCOMMODATIONS:** *Charleston, Empire. Also motels in Coos Bay, North Bend. Write Coos Bay C of C, P.O. Box 210, for brochure listing all area motels.*

from the highway. U.S. 101 wherever it runs inland from the shore is likely to have a lesser, local road west of it, giving access to a beach of some interest.

## Coos Bay and surrounds

To be frank about it, the adjoining towns of Coos Bay and North Bend do little to impress highway travelers with their physical beauty. U.S. 101 winds along the shore of Coos Bay between mills on the water side and the back doors of business on the other. On an overcast day, with mill smoke adding to an already funereal pall, the temptation is to keep on going.

It is not a fair impression. There is a great deal to do for beachcombers of every stripe in surroundings more than passably attractive once west of the highway. The opportunity for tidewater recreation is as richly diverse here as it is anywhere along an Oregon coast with a reputation for variety.

### INSIDE COOS BAY

The bay is a long, narrow body that leans north from its mouth for several miles, then changes its mind and loops way back south. As far as clammers and fishermen are concerned, it is the northward leaning leg that matters.

**Empire** a small town on the bay shore west of Coos Bay town, marks the upper limit of a popular clam bed. Digging is from the pulp mill west for five miles to the mouth of South Slough. The Cape Arago Highway follows the shoreline, making access easy. Gapers and cockles abound about equally in the sand-and-mud tideflats, and it takes fast digging to beat cave-ins of soggy holes. The far shore (North Spit) has even better digging, but the only way to get there is by small boat.

To get to Empire, or any ocean destination, motorists can turn west on Central Avenue in Coos Bay, or Virginia Avenue in North Bend. Both streets connect to Cape Arago Highway.

**Charleston** at the west end of the bridge spanning South Slough, is the biggest small boat basin in the bay. Rental boats and charter boats both operate from this town, huddled along a narrow shelf in the lee of Coos Head. From here, boat fishermen can launch expeditions for striped bass (upper bay and North Slough parallel to the highway bridge, and in South Slough), or for halibut, sole, ling cod, flounder, red snappers, and sea bass in the lower bay. Salmon forays go outside for Chinooks from mid-July to late September and for silvers during July and August.

Crab rings can be rented for use either from boats or from dock areas.

Another activity much pursued by fish widows and their children is the Snug Harbor Railroad, a non-profit, zoo-type line that circles lazily around a loop track laid in dunes along the Charleston waterfront. Commercial fisherman Leonard Hall operates it on every sunny Sunday of the year.

*Spray soars a hundred feet above a towering winter wave at Shore Acres*

## THE OCEAN BEACHES

Outside the south jetty there begins a series of beach parks of varying interest to geologists, clammers, rock and surf fishermen, beachcombers, picnickers, and scenery watchers.

**Bastendorff Beach** stretches from the jetty, the least scenic of the several beaches between the bay mouth and Cape Arago, but no less popular for that. For one thing, razor clams exist in fair numbers in the deep sand at the extreme low tide line. For another, smelt run strongly all through the summer season. For still a third, good drift floats inshore at Bastendorff. On occasion, a local contingent of surfers uses the beach with moderate success. At the south end of the beach, Coos Head cliffs yield up a fair array of Eocene marine fossils.

Picnic and parking facilities are extensive.

**Smelt Beach,** below a bumpy spur road off the Cape Arago Highway just south of the crest south of Bastendorff Beach, enjoys a great reputation among dip-netters for its smelt run. From the end of the road, it is a long, tedious scramble down a slippery path to the pocket cove. Surf fishermen also find the beach worth the difficult climb down and back up again. It is also known locally as Lighthouse Beach, Cape Arago light being visible on the south headland.

**Sunset Bay,** in the lee of the Cape Arago lighthouse point, is the first of three adjoining parks, each with a distinctly individual character. Sunset Bay, wind-sheltered by steep sandstone bluffs that curve out to form a narrow mouth, is both an excellent swimming beach and a fine vantage point for wave-watching. The

lighthouse reservation, accessible to the north, adds another perspective to the latter activity. This is the only park of the three with campsites.

**Shore Acres State Park** to the south used to be the estate of lumber and shipping magnate Asa M. Simpson. In it remain some of the sumptuous and exotic gardens he established, and games courts take considerable space. On exposed bluffs picnic tables are placed to look out to rocky waters offshore. Good rock fishing is to be had in a small cove north of the main park area in calm weather. In winter storms, huge waves batter the shore.

**Cape Arago State Park** the end of the road and 15 miles from Coos Bay, offers a more natural park atmosphere than Shore Acres. The same 40 to 50-foot bluffs of sandstone extend into this park, and the waters offshore are as rock and reef-ridden as those just north. Sea lions use Simpson Reef just offshore as a staging area for antic competitions (there is a turnout north of the main park area, the dress circle for this show ).The tip of North Cove, in the main park area, all craggy rock, yields good catches of Ling cod, kelp greenling, rock bass, sea trout, sculpin, sea perch, snapper, and tom cod. A sandy beach lies inside that tip, and there is another around in South Cove (the point between is the true Cape Arago). Even in summer an occasional agate may turn up in either cove.

Picnic tables flank each side of long step-and-ramp paths down the bluffs from headquarters to the beach. Some lovers of seascapes have a hard time looking away long enough to eat.

Tidepooling is exceptional, but Oregon Fish Commission permits are required of collectors.

# Happy hunting—agates

Along the rainy coast, from Mendocino County in California north to Washington's Cape Flattery, hundreds of short, violent rivers quarry rocks out of their beds and ferry them down to the sea. The sea chips away at rocky bluffs along its own shore. Between them the two forces give rockhounds ample excuse to wander the scenic beaches.

Agates preponderate, and Oregon is far and away the richest source of the semi-precious stones.

On the southern Oregon beaches, gem quality agate, jasper, petrified wood (myrtle mostly), serpentine, and Oregon "jade" (grossularite garnet) can be found in beach gravel. Agatized myrtle, blue and white banded agates, and flower jaspers are most common at the beaches on Seven Devils Road between Coos Bay and Bandon. On the bars of the Illinois and Rogue Rivers and on the strand at Gold Beach, serpentine and Oregon jade are the prime stones.

In central Oregon, where agates are a staple business and hobby, beachwalkers find quality agate, jasper, Oregon jade, and pertified wood. At Road's End, colorful jaspers are the most frequent find. Agates good for tumbling turn up on all the beaches from Newport to Oceanlake, and especially on Agate Beach. Sagenitic agates can be found with fair regularity on the beaches between Yachats and Heceta Head. The same beaches also turn up bloodstones and other jaspers and agates. Some of the most favored locations are the mouths of Big, China, Cummings, Tenmile, and Squaw creeks.

Northern Oregon beaches yield the same run of stones. Beaches near Oceanside have sagenitic agates and some colorful jaspers. Tillamook County beaches seem to hold unusually large specimens.

Winter is the best hunting season because the storms strip sand off the beaches, revealing untouched gravel beds, and because the creeks and rivers run high, washing new stones out to the beaches.

Agates of every stripe have identifying names. Some of them are: Agate or Moonstone agate (brilliantly clear), Carnelian (bright red and translucent), Ribbon (any stone with banded colors), Cloud (clear with dark formations), Moss (clear but containing mineral crystals or other crystallized matter), Chrysoprase (apple-green and translucent), and Iris or Rainbow (refracts seven irridescent colors).

The rarest of all agates is the water agate, a stone which has trapped in it a drop of water with a moving bubble of air. All agates are formed by the seeping of water-borne silica and oxygen into a cavity left by the decay of animal or vegetable matter within sedimentary rock. The result is a massive variety of quartz. It is freak chance that water is trapped during the formation of the stone, although stray mineral matter almost always precipitates along with the silica.

Jasper is formed the same way, but is made opaque by the oxides, clay, and other impurities that color it.

*Sand for summer sunning at Shore Acres*

## LONELY SEVEN DEVILS

Between Coos Bay and Bandon below the old Seven Devils Stage Road, a man can walk for six lonely miles along the shore at low tide, keeping an eye out for agates among the rainbow of rocks that litters the way, and maybe stopping to see if there's anything left of one of Oregon's best gold strikes.

These beaches remain little visited, except by local rockhounds, mainly because the road falls in the rudimentary class for part of the distance. Most of the twisting route is paved from its beginning west of the bridge in Charleston to its junction with U.S. 101 near Bandon. But the shore is accessible only from an unpaved loop that runs west of the main road.

Sacchi's Beach gives the motorist bound south from Charleston his first view of the sea, but the road to it is private and posted.

**Agate Beach** two miles beyond, also private, can be examined for a small fee, and for a slightly larger fee can be used for camping. The spur road down to the camping area is rough, and muddy in winter, but almost always passable. It is here that local rockhounds gather after winter storms to hunt for agates, jasper, and chunks of petrified wood. The cliffs here, the same Eocene sandstone of the state parks on Cape Arago, contain concretions in numbers, and occasionally reveal a marine fossil, usually a forebear of the chambered nautilus.

**Merchant's Beach,** another two miles south, is reached by private road, too. The route is sometimes made impassable by mud in the rainy season. Rockhounding here equals that at Agate Beach in number, quality, and diversity. The difference is that the beach is a good deal longer. At low tide, the rocky headland separating the two beaches can be rounded dryly.

*Chill fog* shrouds Bandon jetty and old lighthouse

*Seastacks* loom out of surf at Bandon

**Whiskey Run Beach,** three more miles south where the road begins to be paved again, had the gold rush. It began in 1853, and the quoted figure is $2 million worth of gold came out of the sand by placer mining. A good number of optimists still try to boost that figure up a bit by panning when they pass by, but most visitors look for agates or decorative bits of driftwood, both abundant at this beach.

A small, rough-hewn camping area is at the end of the wide, gravelled access road, a mile off Seven Devils Road. From there, the beach is another few hundred yards down Whiskey Creek. The hills behind the beach are covered with gorse, a brilliant yellow show in spring bloom, a fire hazard in summer, and a thorny bother to anybody who has to walk through it.

Beachwalkers can round the headland at the north to get back to Merchant's Beach.

From the access road, it is 10 miles south to Bandon, or 15 miles north to Charleston.

# Bandon to Brookings

No road from the Oregon interior joins U.S. 101 south of Bandon to the border. It is 100 miles of some of the quietest coast in these United States in winter, when the tide of tourists ebbs toward absolute zero. At one time, the highway between Port Orford and Brookings terrified hundreds of motorists and their passengers. Some of the latter, in fact, made the trip on the floorboards rather than regard the fog-hazed edge of oblivion just a few feet away from the curve-filled road. They never went back, either.

Since the late 1950's the road has been a fine, fast, well-marked one. Terror has been engineered out of it, leaving motorists a good deal freer to enjoy some of the most scenic mileage of all the Oregon seashore.

## BANDON

Bandon, on the mouth of the Coquille River, ships lumber in substantial quantity, although overshadowed by the Port of Coos Bay, and it is a summer cottage town to boot. Most of the cottage owners flee to Bandon to beat the summer heat at Roseburg, or one of the Willamette Valley towns. They and other visitors share an extensive and extensively varied shoreside terrain.

**Bullards Beach State Park,** north of the town and the north end of the river bridge, has a boat launch on the Coquille River, and gives access to four miles of ocean beach on the north spit of the river.

**Bandon Jetty Park,** beginning alongside the south jetty and extending to the south end of a low, treeless plain, has good rock fishing from the jetty, good surf fishing, and fair clamming for softshells in a low bog well inside the jetty mouth.

The bar at Bandon has a long and gloomy history of sinking lumber vessels, with unpredictable seas and dense fogs about equally responsible. An abandoned light sits forlornly at a point about midway out along the north jetty, mute testimony to a long struggle to tame that bar with jetty extensions. In 1953, the bar caught the aging freighter *Oliver Olson* and cast her onto the tip of the south jetty. She tore out her bottom, jammed her rudder, and fouled her screws. There was no getting her off, but the jetty needed extending anyway, so the salvers filled her holds with rocks and left her where she was, 307 feet of a total extension of 450 feet.

**Bandon Waysides State Park** lies just south of the towering bluff on which much of the residential and cottage area of the town is built, the better to enjoy an eerie view full of tall, thin seastacks of sombre black rock rising above a broad sandy strand. The park is on Bandon

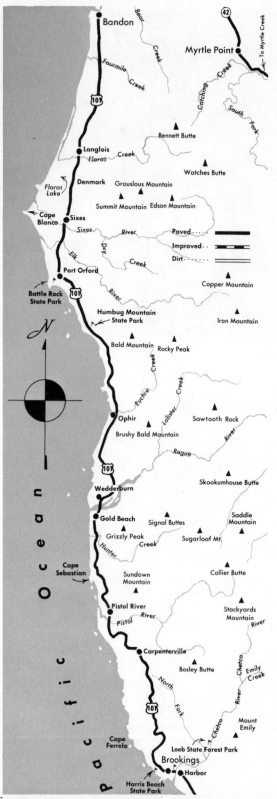

Loop Road, two miles south of this residential area, and can be reached either from town or from a point on U.S. 101 four miles south of town. In contrast to the high bluffs of the privately-held portions of the loop road, the park beach is backed by low dunes that roll away from the shore under a light blanket of shrubby growth.

The surf zone is unusually wide for this part of the coast, and the shoal beach is as productive for surf fishermen as the area near the jetty. A tangle of driftwood marks the surf line of winter storms and contains in it collectable pieces, but it gets a regular working over.

## BETWEEN THE TOWNS

Several famous shoreside points occur in the long drive between Bandon and Brookings. Among them are Cape Blanco, Battle Rock, Humbug Mountain, and Cape Sebastian. It is possible to see, too, how tough this road used to be at Humbug Mountain and farther south from Cape Sebastian to Cape Ferrelo.

**Cape Blanco Lighthouse** sits on a point at the end of a bucolic road that wanders six miles northwestward from its juncture with U.S. 101 six miles north of Port Orford or 23 miles south of Bandon. For the present, this is as far west as an automobile can be driven anywhere along the coast. It is also a famous weather station among the seafaring company of the world, who know it as the southern limit of almost every winter storm that strikes the Pacific Northwest coast. Low pressure areas approach the coast on an exceptionally well-defined track. The storm centers sweep ashore one after another between the Strait of Juan de Fuca and Grays Harbor in Washington. It is monotonous fidelity. When it happens, the weather bureau report reads "Storm warnings are posted from Tatoosh to Cape Blanco for west to southwest winds from 25 to 35 miles per hour." At newspaper offices all over two states copyboys fill in their forms with wind velocity. Good weather vistas are magnificent. Visiting hours are 1-3 p.m. daily, and September is the best month.

**Port Orford** shares its town name with an especially desirable variety of softwood lumber, Port Orford cedar. The town is not, however, a major lumber port. Its small harbor has more fishing vessels in it than any other kind of boat or ship. And a casual harbor it is. Local fishermen sometimes use long sandy beach south of town as an informal boat ways. They run their vessels ashore on a spring tide, block them up, overhaul the hulls, and float them back out on the next spring tide.

**Battle Rock State Park** a hump-backed high-tide islet locked in the curve of the shoreline, was once very handy for settlers, In 1851 when hostile Indians attacked, the settlers retreated to the easily defended island, where they were able to withstand a siege. A narrow footpath leads to the top of the tree-covered island, where children withstand the contemporary sieges of mothers even more easily than the settlers withstood the Indians. Getting on the island is easy at any time except full high tide, when the inner end is washed by surging surf and the tangle of driftwood there gets set into motion.

At low tide, there is a wave tunnel that goes all the way through the rock crossways, and which has a narrow cross tunnel that goes several yards toward the seaward end. It is satisfactorily wet and dark and cold in there.

*SHORESIDE CAMPING: Harris Beach State Park (Brookings) (82 units, 34 trailer units); Humbug Mountain State Park (6 mi. so. of Port Orford) (63 units, 30 trailer units); Bullards Beach State Park (1 mi. no. of Bandon) (128 sites). SHORESIDE ACCOMMODATIONS: Brookings, Gold Beach-Wedderburn, Port Orford, Bandon.*

A parking lot and some rustic picnic tables are at the side of U.S. 101 on the south side of the Port Orford business district. So is a sign explaining the battle.

**Humbug Mountain State Park** circles the steep flanks of the mountain that towers up from the horizon south of Port Orford. Most of the park is on the sheltered inland side of the conical mountain, but on the north side trails lead from a turnout down to a fine, sandy beach cut in two by the pleasant creek that keeps companiably alongside the road for miles.

Aside from the beach area, there are trails from the camping area out to the seaward side of the mountain for panoramic views.

The distance from Port Orford is about six miles.

**Geisel Monument State Park** is mainly a picnic area at the roadside between the tiny town of Ophir on the south and Humbug Mountain on the north. North of the turnout, a long beach of black sand stretches away beneath the bluffs that mark the beginning of rolling hills which continue to the mountain, hiding the sea from view all the while.

**Gold Beach** and its companion town Wedderburn sit on either side of the Rogue River mouth 55 miles north of the California border and 78 miles south of Coos Bay. The local fame rests on this being the downstream end of the Rogue River mailboat run, a bucketing diversion which has gained such popularity that other boats follow the same course at competitive prices and still others go farther for more.

The local beach is no slouch either. It is a long, wide, sandy affair with gravelly patches for agate hunters, and an endless line of driftwood to be examined for something attractive enough to cart home. It's a long walk from the highway, but south of the business district several access roads dip down to the back of a narrow line of dunes to ease that burden. This sand is coarse stuff, and it is no good forcing the issue with an automobile. The local towing firm does a brisk annual business with novices who push their luck too far because the sand looks just as inviting as the finer stuff farther north.

The summer surf line is farther away than the winter from the road, and there is a wave-eroded little shelf about two feet high that cups and catches sand dollar and snail shells as well as agates during the summer. A similar but shorter beach is accessible through Wedderburn.

The deservedly popular boat trips leave from both the Gold Beach and Wedderburn sides of the river, daily at 8.30 or 9 a.m. in summer, and on Mondays, Wednesdays, and Fridays from Wedderburn only in winter. The Wedderburn boat is the genuine mail carrier. It is a 54-mile, all-day round-trip up a green and steep-sided Rogue River canyon. Wild animals populate the river banks between the bottom of the river and Agness, the top end of the run, where lunch is possible if not a downright necessity to survival.

**Cape Sebastian State Park** eight-plus miles south of Gold Beach, is there to take advantage of the view. It does. Two beaches north and south are pleasant, and served by turnouts with paths leading down shallow bluffs to broad, sandy strands. But Cape Sebastian is the seaward side of a towering mountain that crests 1722 feet above sea level. The 700 feet to the top of the cape approaches the vertical.

*Agate hunter stalks Gold Beach*

*Settlers held out on Battle Rock in 1851*

*Driftwood hunt around Battle Rock today*

At the summit of U.S. 101, a spur road leads west, higher up the cape. It forks, one spur leading to an overlook on the north shoulder of the peak, the other spur leading still higher to an overlook that takes in the ocean horizon as well as an enormous expanse of coastline to the south. From here, a footpath goes yet higher to a windswept, sparsely blanketed knob-knoll that gives unobstructed vision in all directions and befuddles cameras. At the bottom of the access road, a sign advises that cars with trailers should not essay the climb. It means it. The grind is first-gear all the way up.

**Pistol River** gives overheated radiators a chance to cool at sea level between high climbs north and south, and it further has a fine expanse of sandy beach where an amplitude of driftwood invites exploration. The north end of the beach is beset, scenically, with several seastacks. A lagoon of usually brackish water complicates the crossing of the sand, but not beyond solution. According to one local expert, the last excitement was in 1856 when Indians attacked a small colony of settlers, resulting in the explosive name of the community and its eventual selection as a historical landmark.

## BROOKINGS

The last outpost of coastal Oregon is Brookings, a pleasant town with an assortment of scenic distinctions to its credit, as well as some of the most productive waters in the state for salmon and crab fishermen.

The pleasant aspect of the town owes itself largely to a year-around display of flowers. Lilies in commercial fields bloom in July, and in January acres of daffodils blossom. In addition to these, Azalea State Park on the east edge of town has a rare collection of its namesake plant within its boundaries, and Loeb State Park, seven miles east of U.S. 101 on the Chetco River north bank, is graced by a virgin stand of Myrtlewood trees.

It is the multi-faceted shore, though, that offers the greatest scenic beauty and opportunity for recreation.

**Samuel H. Boardman State Park** occupies an 11-mile-long area that, in its time, supported the most harrowing curves of a highway filled with trauma for first-timers on it. In this enlightened era of highway engineering, the road is mainly thought of as a convenient way to get to Lone

Ranch, Whale's Head, and other shore areas of the park.

The southern edge of the park is five miles north of Brookings, where a spur road drops down to Lone Ranch. On rare occasions, a chunk of pricite turns up in the sand to remind the knowledgeable beachwalker that the area was once a borax mine. Those days are gone forever, and the beach now serves mainly as a backdrop to picnics, or a good spot to try casting into the surf for sea perch and the like, or a place to dig butter clams.

Another four miles north, Whale's Head reveals the reason for its name when the tide is right, and an offshore rock "blows" in proper Cetacean fashion. The rock is visible from the highway, but a spur road leads to a picnic area next to a fine, sandy beach from where the rock appears more whale-like.

Arch Rock (also known as Windy Point) lies just north of the Thomas Creek Bridge, one of the statistical wonders of the area. The bridge is 345 feet from creek bed to deck, about two hands higher than the Golden Gate. Arch Rock also has a picnic area.

Lofty viewpoints are at several turnouts between the beaches. One of these, Houserock Viewpoint between Lone Ranch and Whales Head, allows sunny day visitors to see south to Point St. George off Crescent City, California, and north to Cape Sebastian.

**Harris Beach State Park** on the north edge of town two miles from the middle of the business district, has both sandy and rocky stretches of shoreline. The sandy stretch lies mainly to the north of the main parking lot. Hardy types swim in the surf on incoming tides (bars offshore set up strong longshore and rip currents on the outgoing tides). Surf fishermen work the beach heavily, too. Picnic tables ring the parking lot, looking out to sea rather than back at all that machinery.

To the south of the parking lot, a knobby little headland seems to close off the beach. It doesn't. There is a trail over one shoulder of it that leads down to a tiny cove that is one, enormous tidepool at low tide. Waves come through a hole in the rock that forms the offshore side of the cove, and swell out in a flawless, 180° ring. It is a somewhat startling sight to see, and it keeps enormous populations of Hermit crabs, assorted snails, and sea anemones supplied with items of fresh interest. Harris Beach is a preserve. The collecting of intertidal animals is limited to holders of permits issued by the state to legitimate students of marine biology. But it is still enjoyable to poke about in this and adjoining pools to the south, and conchologists will find a fair supply of uninhabited shells.

The offshore Goat Island, in spite of its name, is a refuge for sea birds.

**Mill Beach** west of the Brookings Plywood Mill and accessible by way of Mill Beach Road, attracts tidepoolers and rock fishermen.

Another beach on the north side of the Chetco River Jetty has agates and other stones of interest to rockhounds. The road parallel to and behind the beach is called Memory Lane.

**Sporthaven** on the south side of the river at the inner end of the jetty, has both charter boats for offshore salmon and bottom fishing, and a county launching ramp. The beach outside Sporthaven and south of the jetty is also good rockhounding territory.

# The scenic central coast

Mile for mile, the mid-section of Oregon is the most wildly various segment of a coast that is famous for its beauty and for the variety of beauty.

It has towering mountains that pitch steeply into the sea; craggy sections of rock that tower less high but create pounding, turbulent surf; long stretches of low-lying sand; small harbors that might well scare the whiskers off a Newfoundland cod fisherman, and, unique in all the world, a fleet of sand dunes of such scope as to defy comparison.

In all that variety, the opportunity for shoreside diver-sion is as great as logic might demand. The number of resort towns organized to make the best of a good thing is commensurate. At one or another of them, there is the possibility of clamming, crabbing, smelting, rockhounding, tidepooling, driftwood hunting or general beachcombing, skin diving, surf fishing, deep sea fishing, storm watching, or lighthouse collecting, to say nothing of swimming or heading out for an exploratory trip aboard a dunes buggy.

## The Dunes Coast

From the town of Florence, U.S. 101 for 49 miles south-cuts through the famous Oregon sand dunes or close along behind them. Pushed along by the strong coastal winds, the sand blows up the beach, then inland as an almost inexorable force.

Naturalist Ivan T. Sanderson described the dunes: " . . . they are veritable sand mountains which at some points extend for more than two miles back from the sea and rise to a height of some three hundred feet. The sand is forever moving inland and trailing off to the northeast. It follows the normal behavior of dunes, but on such a grandiose scale that it produces some astonishing results. First, low down by the sea, there are just normal dunes, but behind these are vast masses of sand sculpted around outlying blocks of vegetation that somehow have been able to withstand their onslaught, and that now lie in smoothly curved bowls and funnels, the tops of their tallest trees being below the level of the sand all around."

For all the length of these dunes, only a few points give easy access, and only a few more give rather more difficult admittance. Florence is the handy end for walking around in the sand. Hauser, just a few miles north of Coos Bay, is the center of activity for dunes buggies, stripped down cars of a certain age that go out on the roller coaster slopes in complete safety and permit luxuriously easy exploration.

### THE BEACHES NEAR FLORENCE

On the north side of the Siuslaw River, the sand continues unabated, but the shoreline west of Florence has been largely stabilized. Two parks, one on the river and the other on the ocean shore, are pleasant in themselves and have the further advantage of being surrounded on all sides by a magnificent stand of rhododendrons.

**Florence** has a small boat harbor tucked along a nar-row shelf on the north bank of the Siuslaw River east of the U.S. 101 highway bridge. Charter boats put out over the bar for Chinook salmon from May until August, and again in mid-September. The run of silvers in this harbor begins with the fall rains, peaks in October and November, and trails off gradually through December.

**Harbor Vista Park** looks out over the river mouth and jetties, from a point four miles west of town. Picnic tables and campsites are on a bluff, sheltered from sea winds by wax myrtle and shore pines. The undergrowth to these consists mainly in rhododendrons, which bloom in mid-May and perfume the salt air with another, sweeter frag-rance. Trails lead down from the bluffs to the river edge,

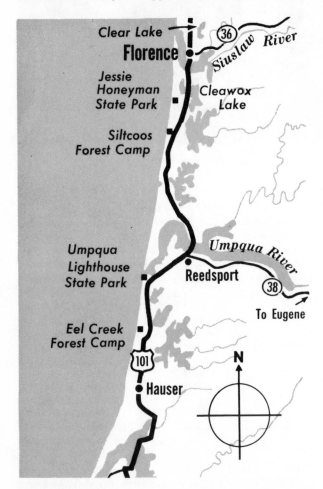

*SHORESIDE CAMPING: Eel Creek Forest Camp (15 mi. no. of North Bend) (10 units, 89 trailer units); Umpqua Light State Park (6 mi. so. of Reedsport) (41 units, 22 trailer units); between Reedsport and Florence, south to north, are Tahkenitch Lake Forest Camp (4 units, 32 trailer units); Carter Lake Forest Camp (2 units, 20 trailer units); Siltcoos Lake Forest Camp (35 units, 61 trailer units); Honeyman State Park (240 units, 66 trailer units); Siuslaw Harbor Vista County Park (20 units, 18 trailer units); Sutton Lakes Forest Camp (6 mi. no. of Florence) (14 units, 79 trailer units). SHORESIDE ACCOMMODATIONS: Winchester Bay has three motels. Inshore, Reedsport, and Florence have greater numbers. No lists available.*

*Footprints lead over the dunes near Florence. Hauser dunes buggy is easier way to go*

and a public road continues west from the park to the jetty area, where fishing is good for sea perch, sea trout, and sea bass.

A drive out this road on the night of a rolling, tumbling sea fog is one of the world's eeriest motoring trips. Whole stands of trees have died beneath encroaching sands, and car headlights probing into these stark and twisted tangles of dead wood give any viewer cause to wonder what is out there. An ensuing grove of healthy vegetation restores a semblance of reality to the landscape, then the road turns another hillock and the world goes grotesque again.

It is better to try this road on a foggy night than others in the area, because the others heading into the dunes have fewer guidelines to keep a driver oriented. Anybody who drives into the sand will jolly well stay there until a tow truck can be summoned to the rescue.

**Heceta Beach Park** a picnic park on a broad and sandy beach, shares the area with a number of summer homes. A wide surf zone holds within it a fair number of surf fish, the major attraction of the beach.

## SOUTH TO COOS BAY

**South Jetty Road** tacks west off U.S. 101 from the crest of the hill south of Glenada, the small town on the south side of the Siuslaw River. It offers the longest look for the least effort from an automobile or on foot, as it goes over the high crest of the dunes, then cuts northwest across an incredibly wide and rolling expanse of sand. The road is posted for slow speeds because the sand keeps encroaching on it, and it goes as its name indicates all the way to the river mouth, where a large parking lot gives access to a fishing platform at the inner end of the jetty,

and to the ocean beach a few hundred yards away by well-defined but shifty trail. It is a quick and easy introduction to sand walking, and will demonstrate what longer trips through this finely granulated stuff would be like.

**Jessie Honeyman State Park,** three miles south of Florence, and a good headquarters from which a camper might explore, has within its boundaries two dunes-beset lakes. Cleawox lies entirely within the park, and Woahink borders it. The lakes are at least partly backward in orientation. The sand has left thick stands of trees and brush on the west shores, while the east shores are sand deserts rolling away to sudden horizon lines. Trails lead through the scrubby growth west of the Cleawox Lake, and on to the shore. The easiest way to keep oriented (and it is not easy) is to follow the stream from its outlet on the north side of the lake. (Stay with the stream to avoid a bog due west of the lake.) Honeyman, partly because of the swimming lakes, is usually crowded as a camping park.

**Siltcoos Forest Camp** one of dozens of pleasant camping parks in the Siuslaw National Forest, sits at the end of a spur road that ends just a half a mile from the ocean shore. From it, the stroll across the dunes is considerably shorter than the one at Honeyman, and leaves more energy for hikers to comb the beach for sand dollar shells far north or south of the mouth of the creek that courses from the camp to the sea. The entry point is on U.S. 101 seven miles south of Florence.

**Carter Lake** (West) a short distance south virtually repeats Siltcoos, except that there is fishing in the stream at Siltcoos and little of it here.

**Tahkenitch Lake** to the south of Carter Lake, does not

*Picnic or just sit at Harbor Vista Park. Sandy east shore of swimmable Lake Woahink*

offer easy access to the ocean. The interest here is in the good fishing in the lake itself, and in swimming in its waters when the sun warms them. It is a forest service camp, too.

**Reedsport** a town with bravery enough to paint a pun in huge letters on the facade of its high school, sits at the head of Winchester Bay, which enjoys considerable local reputation for being a fine crabbing and salmon fishing area. The small town of **Winchester Bay** is on the south side near the harbor mouth. The small boat harbor, called Salmon Harbor, is near Winchester Bay town, and is most active in July, August, and September, when Chinooks and silvers show up outside the bar and start to move inside.

**Umpqua Lighthouse State Park** (Umpqua is the name of the river flowing through this bay) sits on the coast just south of the bay mouth and draws as much attention as the dunes, in easy hiking distance south of the light and the park around it. Little Lake Marie has picnic sites of considerable charm when the weather is good.

**William Tugman State Park** and **Eel Creek Forest Camp** to the west of Ten Mile Lakes (good trolling for salmon at the creek mouth and in the lakes during the spring tides of the month of October), nestles in a grove of salal, wax myrtle, manzanita and shore pines. A trail leads for 400 yards through this typical vegetation of the Oregon coast, and emerges on the back side of the dunes a mile and a half from the shore. The hardy can hike across a whole series of sand hills and sand valleys to the sea. It is a good idea to mark the trail with one or more bright bits tied to snags or scrub growth on the crests of some of these hills. They all look alike otherwise.

**Hauser** has the dunes buggies, which cruise the dunes at a top speed of 35 miles per hour, stop for photographers, and offer a choice of the whole scenic trip to the shore or a shorter roller-coaster trip among the steepest dunes. The price for either is small.

Hauser is nine miles north of Coos Bay.

Cameras hauled along on trips into the dunes here or elsewhere should be kept in an air-sealed plastic bag, between pictures or sand will sift into the shutter assembly almost certainly.

## The craggy middle

North of Florence as far as Newport, the coast of Oregon is mainly steep hills and craggy rocks. It is but lightly populated, partly because of the tough terrain, partly because the Siuslaw National Forest covers more than half of this shore area and no towns can be built in it, terrain or no.

### IN THE FOREST

Immediately north of Florence, the coastal shelf ceases to look like dunes country, although there are episodic fleets of the moving hills all the way to Waldport. For a few miles, it ceases being a shelf at all in a cataclysmic change of character.

**Sea Lion Caves,** 11 miles north of Florence or 39 miles south of Newport, is a natural wonder on at least two scores.

# Is it a seal or sea lion?

*Harbor seal behind sea lion*

Four seal or seal-like animals frequent the Pacific shore from Canada to Mexico, occasionally joined by another two species more or less similar in appearance. All of them tend to be called seals. They are not all the same kind.

Two species of true seals and four of eared seals (including two sea lions) are native to the coastal waters of this continent. All belong to a sub-order of flesh-eating mammals called *Pinnipedia* (fin-footed) because all have fins rather than legs. The important difference is that the eared seals have mobile hindquarters.

A sea lion can rotate his hind flippers from back to front. They are usually pointed to the front, alongside the body, when the animal rests on a beach or rock. (The two rare species along the U.S. coast, the Guadalupe and Alaskan fur seals, are related to sea lions, but are so seldom seen they do not pose a great problem of identification.)

The true seals have flippers fixed in a position behind the body like a tail.

In thumbnail, the four frequently seen animals are:

The Steller sea lion is the big, boisterous animal that ranges from the Bering Sea to California's Channel Islands. Its coat is a tawny brown-yellow loosely wrapped about a frame that reaches as many as 12 feet in length. Top weight is about a ton for a bull. Cows reach nine feet in length and 700 pounds top weight. They live to an age of about 20 years, can dive to depths of 100 fathoms and remain submerged for as many as five minutes. Using a straight breaststroke, the sea lion can hit a top speed of 17 miles per hour for short stretches. Although it can catch gamefish, and does from time to time, the sea lion seems to prefer a diet of more sluggish fish.

While inlanders tend to say the voice of the coyote is the most melodious sound of them all, a fair share of coast dwellers argue for the resonant bellow of the Steller sea lion. The best places to hear the latter in full song are Sea Lion Caves, and in San Francisco where the native herd members are legal residents of the city and the source of technically incorrect nicknames for a defunct baseball team and an extant hockey club (The Seals, naturally). Seal Rock and Bird Rock in Monterey are other good bets.

The California sea lion ranges from the Washington coast to central Mexico, though seldom much north of San Francisco. This is the performing seal of circuses, zoos, and marine shows. A big specimen reaches eight feet and weighs 1,000 pounds. The bark is a short, sharp honk. It has a poodle-like knot above the forehead, an easy distinction compared to the smoothly sloping brow of the Steller.

The harbor seal (also known as the hair seal and the leopard seal) lives up to its three names. It tends to stay in protected waters. Its fore-flippers are indeed hairy, and its short, fat body has spots to suit a leopard.

It is the smallest pinniped of this coast at 250 pounds and a maximum length of five feet. It is a true seal (the distinguishing mark of the family being a lack of external ears).

The elephant seal is, contrarily, the largest pinniped of the coast, reaching lengths of 17 feet and weights of 5,000 pounds. Any lack of ear is more than compensated in the long, elephantine proboscis which curls down over the mouth of the male. In anger, the bull curls that huge nose against his palate and roars a resonant roar audible for miles under good conditions.

The animal was hunted nearly to extinction during the nineteenth century. Now protected, it is regaining its natural numbers. It is seldom seen except on offshore islands off southern California.

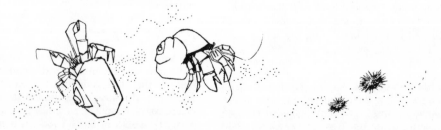

*Dramatic light* at Heceta Head has state parks on either flank

The cave is the world's largest known sea cave. Wave action tunneled 1000 feet through this basaltic headland, apparently working on layers of soft volcanic ash that add to the color of the rocks within.

It is the only known mainland rookery of the Steller sea lion on the American continent.

Sea Lion Caves is a commercial establishment, and has been since 1932. Its owners have guarded the interests of the sea lions with care at the same time they have worked out points from which visitors can look closely into the impolitely fascinating habits of these bulky beasts. The two main areas are a roofed shed that looks down to an open ledge where most of the animals spend most of their time, and the balcony in the cave itself.

**Heceta Head Light** visible just north of the Sea Lion Caves curio shop and parking lot, can be visited only by appointment, and only by organized groups. Its photogeneity is indisputable.

**Devils Elbow State Park** occupies the south side of the head and a small crescent beach below the light tower. The park has picnic facilities. The rock fishing is not bad, except that the neighboring sea lions are generally more skilled at it than any human competitor, and a man can get an inferiority complex trying.

**Washburne State Park** occupies the other side of Heceta Head. One of the newest of the Oregon state parks in 1965, it has a longer beach than Devils Elbow, and there is safe swimming in addition to surf fishing. A walk back toward Heceta Head to some gravelly patches of beach may turn up agates at the price of a patient search. This park has picnic facilities, too.

**Ponsler Memorial Wayside,** the next park in a steady string of them, is a mile north of Washburne. Its charms are those of its neighbors, with the added advantage that the road swoops down nearly to sea level, permitting easier access to a long, clean beach of sand in summer and pebbles in winter. China Creek flows between the Washburne and Ponsler beaches, and is the source of the pebbles which include a fair number of agates. Somehow, most of them seem to wind up south of the creek mouth, but there are always a few north of it.

**Ocean Beach Park,** a forest service campground, should get a prize for being the most directly named geographic point in the state. Whether it does or not, it is the most southerly of a string of good smelt beaches that extends north to Yachats. The park has a picnic area. South of it, near the mouth of Rock Creek, is a good beach for con-chologists to poke about in search of the usual run of coldwater shells.

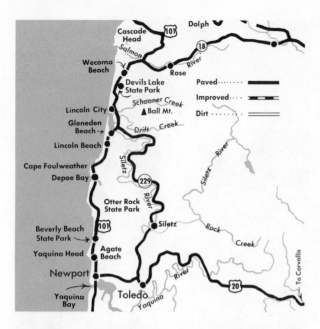

**SHORESIDE CAMPING:** *Between Heceta Head and Newport, from south to north, are Carl Washburne State Park (58 trailer units); Neptune State Park (14 units); Cape Perpetua Forest Camp (42 units); Tillicum Beach Forest Camp (7 units, 40 trailer units); Beachside State Park (60 units, 20 trailer units); Beverly Beach State Park (7 mi. no. of Newport) (155 units, 129 trailer units); Devils Lake State Park (68 units, 32 trailer units).* **SHORESIDE ACCOMMODATIONS:** *Yachats has several, no list available. Newport has many; write Newport C of C, 555 S.W. Coast Highway, Newport, 97365, for list. Taft to Oceanlake area has nearly 100. Write Twenty Miracle Miles Ad Club, Box 604, Lincoln City, for list.*

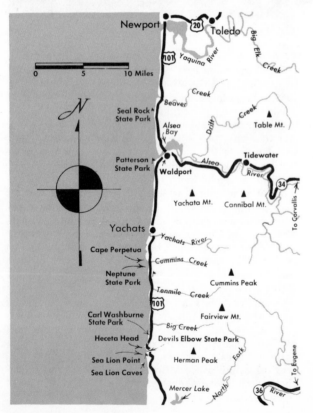

The next smelt beach is not in a park. It is along the shore between Squaw Creek (the first creek north of Ocean Beach) and Ten Mile Creek. The area around the mouth of Ten Mile Creek is also good for agates.

**Neptune State Park,** five and a half desolate miles north of Ocean Beach or four miles south of Yachats, is not a big park, but it has several aspects of its beach worth investigating. Long flat fingers of rock poke out into the surf zone to make good staging areas for rock fishermen. The same rocks harbor sizable colonies of rock oysters (alias piddock clams), a nourishing addition to seafood stews, and a challenge to pry out of the rock with hammer and chisel. Or, tidepoolers can expect to find giant green anemones, starfish, mussels, and all their ecological associates.

Down on the sandy stretch of the beach, gravel patches yield a fair number of agates.

Like its mates, this park has picnic sites.

**Cape Perpetua,** a forest service campground a mile and a half north, extends the accessible shoreline without changing its character. It too has a sizeable picnic ground. From it a spur road leads up 800 feet to the top of the cape, from whence an awesome panorama unfolds.

Down at the mouth of Cape Creek, the **Devil's Churn** is a deep trough in the rocky shore, where winter waves boil into violent spray above an unusually turbulent surface of the sea. The climb is steep.

This whole length of coast with its long, flat tongues of rock bounding the shore is a great place for wave watching summer and winter, but when a December norther comes along the surf mounts to genuinely spectacular furies.

## TOWNS AND TAMER WATERS

Cape Perpetua is the last nod of Siuslaw National Forest to a northbound beachcomber until he comes to a rump section of the forest north of Oceanlake. The 22 miles from Yachats to Newport has several towns oriented mainly toward summer cottages, salmon fishermen, and other outdoorsmen.

**Yachats,** long a slumbering village of no especial note, blossomed during the 1950s into a fairly vigorous resort community. Its proximity to the wilderness south, its unusually heavy smelt run, and its good river fishing combined to give it the boost.

**Yachats State Park** fronts on the sea on both sides of the Yachats River. Its south half lies westward of a flock of motels. Its north half is west of the town's small business district, below a cottage-covered bluff.

The south half, all rocky, has a long series of tidepools that always seem to have one end still in the frothing surf. In them are some enormous green anemones. These vague looking animals deserve some respect of by-passing humans. For one thing, the biggest ones may be as old as 150 years, no mean accomplishment in a violent neighborhood. For another, one of their number was observed to have eaten a leopard shark (it was, granted, a big anemone vs. a very small shark) as the concluding act of a rough fight.

The river mouth fills with sand in the course of the summer, becoming a fine swimming beach and the site of a major run of silver smelt after June. In winter, the whole thing washes out to sea as the Yachats River swells toward flood stage.

On the beaches farther north, rock and surf fishing are fairly productive. Some sand lingers the year around at the foot of these bluffs, and it contains a few cockles and a very few razor clams.

**Tillicum Beach** a forest service campground, is a mile north of Yachats.

**Beachside State Park,** five miles north of Yachats, comes at the end of a long line of summer home developments. The surf is not safe for swimming, but Big Creek forms a kind of lagoon that is. Surf fishing is good, there are a few razors for clammers to hunt down in the long, wide and sandy beach.

**Patterson State Park** a beach and picnic area, offer some surf fishing, and the hope of razor clams on a minus tide. It is the headland at the mouth of Alsea Bay, just west of the fishing town of Waldport.

**Waldport,** a clean coast town of a certain age, flanks Alsea Bay, a center for salmon fishermen, clammers, and crab fishermen. The salmon fishermen stay inside the river mouth for the good reason that the water outside is too rough and current-ridden for small boats. Crabs in this bay stay alongside the channel and near the mouth. The rocky beaches at and outside the mouth have beds of littlenecks, and in the soft rocks piddock clams. Inside the bay, in the sandy mud are gapers (the local name is horse clam), and blue points (softshells). On the clean sand exposed to the full onslaught of the surf are a few small beds of razor clams.

It is 16 miles from Waldport to Newport, which has a similarly well-endowed bay, and three parks allow the weary traveler to stop and stretch his legs.

**Seal Rock Wayside,** five miles from Waldport, has picnic sites and fishing from a rocky shore. The lush vegetation on the hills, the rocky surf zone, and the trio of Seal Rocks offshore create a pleasant panorama. Its beauty is not the overwhelming sort of the steep sections of the coast, and on the other side is not the gently bucolic kind either.

A small town adjoins the park, consisting in a store, a service station, a post office, and the few residences needed to support these enterprises.

**Ona Beach State Park** halfway between Waldport and Newport, centers on Beaver Creek. The creek swimming hole and picnic area minimize visitor interest in a fine sandy beach just a few yards away, and causes the agate-dotted ocean shore to be surprisingly uncrowded.

**Lost Creek State Park** to the north of Ona Beach, resembles it on the ocean side. Picnic sites at it are pleasantly sheltered from ocean breezes.

## Twenty Miracle Miles?

North of Newport, the flanking towns from Depoe Bay to Oceanlakes advertise themselves as Oregon's "Twenty Miracle Miles." The definition of miracle remains open to question, but the towns thus advertised (and Newport, too) have established their charms beyond doubt in the minds of thousands who come to visit them each year.

Except for Newport's great shipping volume of lumber

*Surf boils* ashore at Neptune State Park

*Sea anemones* under scrutiny at Yachats

*Scavenging gulls* flock after food at Yachats

*Yaquina Head light has all the modern touches. The old light is a museum of the old way*

products and the commercial fishing fleets there and at Depoe Bay and Taft, none of these towns has another significant industry than tourism. It is a scenic chunk of coast with good fishing, rockhounding, tidepooling, clamming, and crabbing to go along with its expanses of sunbathing beach.

## NEWPORT TO BOILER BAY

Second largest shipping port in the world for lumber products, and the only port of consequence between Coos Bay and the Columbia River mouth, Newport enjoys a busy maritime life. As its name suggests, it once attempted to emulate its Atlantic Coast namesake when the latter had more to do with society and less with jazz festivals.

**Bay Front** below the highway bridge, has half a dozen charter services and boat rental agencies where fishermen can equip themselves for salmon fishing outside the harbor mouth (Chinooks and Silvers from May through September) or in the bay (during August), or several other fish. Cod abound in the bay mouth between the jetties, and so do sea bass. Perch and flounder can be caught in the big loop of the upper bay near shore. Local softshell clam beds and oysters are on the tideflats of that same loop, and gapers and cockles are in the cove east of the spit that sticks out from the south shore toward the bay front. Ring fishing for crabs is best from boats just off the bay front piers, along the edge of the channel.

**The Marine Science Center** of Oregon State University is on the south side of the river, its striking aquarium available to public inspection, and well worth it.

**Old Yaquina Bay Lighthouse** dark since 1874 and a museum since 1955, looks out from a steep bluff over the north jetty. The lighthouse building is restored, within limits, to its early functional appearance. Picnic tables scattered about in groves of pine trees, and steep trails down to the jetty and a sandy beach north of it complete a pleasant state park, accessible west of the highway on a road that loops around and under the bridge for northbound motorists.

**Agate Beach** between two and three miles north of Newport, has exposed gravel along its shore the year around. It is the summer vacationer's best hope for finding agates. The small collection of buildings that make up the town sits on a bluff to the west of the highway. Several spur roads give access to the beach. Rockhounds by the score use them.

**Yaquina Head Lighthouse** poses for photographers on a rocky headland to the north of Agate Beach. A loop road connects with U.S. 101. Visiting hours at the 95-foot-tall tower are weekends 1-4 p.m. the year around, and 1-3 p.m. daily in summer. The light is just three miles from the center of Newport.

**Beverly Beach State Park's** sandy strand lies just inshore of a reef that parallels the beach, and takes enough of the sting out of summer surf to allow swimming by anybody hardy enough to endure the water.The beach is thoroughly exposed to shore winds, but picnic facilities and the rest of the amenities are in groves of trees on the inland side of the highway. The park is four miles north of Newport.

A mile north of the park, U.S. 101 starts its long grind

# Catching fresh crabs with rings or rakes

In deep water, crab rings are the only way to come up with the Dungeness crab (Cancer magister as he is formally known). In shallow bays and coastal crab holes, he can be chased with a rake, or a pitchfork, or with bare hands.

Ring fishing for crabs is popular and rewarding in a number of Oregon's bays (Coos, Yaquina, Nestucca, Netarts, Tillamook and Nehalem). In each case the lower bay is the best bet because crabs avoid fresh water, and the ledges where the channels deepen tend to be most productive because crabs gather along them to wait for tidal currents or stream flow to drift food past them.

Minimum tides (neaps) are best for both crabs and crabbers. Food is moving slowly enough for the crab to catch it. Currents out toward the bar are not so strong as to wash a small boat out into the breakers. A novice at boating in these bays should fish only on slack and incoming tides, or should hire a locally knowledgeable pilot to avoid this specific hazard.

Crab rings are constructed to lie flat on the bottom, but to form a basket when they are raised. A line leads from the ring to a cork buoy. Each fisherman can run three traps (the law allows no more), which are baited with scrap fish or fish or shellfish remains. Bait has to be fixed securely to the top side of the netting in order to keep the crab occupied in the ring, and the rings dropped overside so they will sink without flopping over.

The excellent scenting mechanism of the crab will, it is hoped, lead him to the baited trap, which is left in position a maximum of 20 minutes.

To pick up traps, the boat operator approaches against the current for control, and a second person grabs or gaffs the float, then pulls the ring up quickly with a steady hand-over-hand motion to prevent the crabs' escape.

In shallow bays, crabbers can wander along in the shoals in search of crabs feeding beneath the cover of eel grass. The bottom has to be of clean sand or gravel for crabs to gather, and they will not go near a fresh water or industrial waste outlet. The water has to be quiet, too.

Bare-handed crabbers decoy with one hand, and grab the crab from dead astern with the other. There is less risk of being pinched if a rake or pitchfork does the luring job instead. A threatened crab will turn to do battle with the rake, which he will seize as it comes within claw range. All the crabber has to do then is lift the crab out of the water and dump it into a carrying bucket.

Rakes or pitchforks must have the tines covered with tape or rubber tubes so they will not pierce the crabs' shells (it being illegal to spear them).

*Crabber* brings up a ring full

On open coasts crabs sometimes feed in the troughs between sandbars, and get caught in them on ebbing tides. These "crab holes" can be dangerous when a strong ebb occurs (one of several shore currents called "undertow"). Such holes should be scouted for two or three turns of the tide to see how the currents set up. The long handled rake or pitchfork that allows the crabber to stay in shallow water is in order. The best tides are neap tides that begin to ebb just before dawn.

Whether ring or rake crabbing, only the male can be kept. Sexual distinction is easy. The male has a narrow V-plate folded under his stern. The female has a wide one. Legal minimum size is measured across the width of the top shell just ahead of two opposed small points. Legal minimums vary from 5¾ inches to 6¼ inches. A local check on regulations will assure legality.

In bays May seems to be the most productive month. Crabs molt their shells in September and October, during which time the meat is watery and less than appetizing. Taking of soft shell crabs is generally prohibited.

Fresh-caught crabs should be boiled in sea water for 20 minutes, having been pitched into the boiling water while still alive.

up the steep flank of Cape Foulweather. There is no way to escape the climb, but it can be made more profitable by taking the scenic Otter Crest Scenic Loop Road, west of the highway.

**Devil's Punchbowl State Park** a bit less than a mile from the south junction, gets better as the weather gets worse. The reason for the park's existence lies in the presence of a huge, bowl-like cavern fashioned by waves. Two holes in its walls let waves surge up inside it, then subside again. The punch is pure seawater, but it froths fit for a witch.

The town of Otter Rock, adjacent to the park, extends a rocky shoreline that has an extraordinary population of intertidal and other marine animals. The two together make up much of the Marine Gardens, which extend as a posted preserve as far north as Cape Foulweather. The harvesting of any animal from this preserve is forbidden, with no exceptions.

**Otter Crest** near the north end of the scenic road, 500 feet above the sea, has a pullout for panoramic viewing of the coast north and south, and offshore rocks with colonies of "sea lions, sea turkeys, and Oregon penguins."

**Rocky Creek State Park** toward the base of the cape on its north side, consists mainly in a parking lot off U.S. 101 and a trail down to Whale Cove. Picnic sites allow a leisurely contemplation of the seascape, and the rocky cove is good territory for both rock and surf fishermen.

**Depoe Bay** town and park, harbors a sizable fishing fleet in a small bay that often goes unnoticed by non-stop tourists whose attention is riveted on the open cove west of the highway. The boat harbor on the inland side of the highway (access is by a rocky channel under the highway bridge) is colorful. But for sheer drama it cannot compare to the battering surf in the cove when a sea horn spouts water as many as 100 feet in the air (and, when the wind is right, makes this the only undersea passage on the entire highway). The horn isn't always spouting, but when even a moderate sea is running, the cove boils with white water and flying spray.

A private aquarium near the sea horn contains well-presented exhibits of most of the sea animals of the region, and, further, is a dry place from which to observe the waves on a stormy day.

Charter boats from the harbor take all-day fishing excursions and half-hour offshore tours for sightseers when the sea permits.

**Boiler Bay** a mile north of Depoe Bay, and 15 miles north of Newport, got its name from an unromantic accident suffered by an unromantic vessel. In 1910 a crewman on the steam schooner *J. Marhoffer* was trying to patch the ship's coffee pot with an open flame. He set fire to the engine room instead. The skipper sighed deep sighs, abandoned his upcoast course and ran for the beach. The wooden hull burned altogether, but the boiler survived. It lingers in the bay today, visible from time to time on a low tide. The coffee pot melted in the general conflagration.

A small state park overlooks the rockbound cove. From it, grey whales can be sighted on their seasonal treks to and from the Baja California breeding grounds. Rock fishing in the cove is good.

**Fogarty Creek State Park** a mile north of Boiler Bay offers picnickers a set of sheltered stoves on which to heat food as well as a wide, sandy beach safe for swimming and

productive of surf fish. The picnic sites are on the east side of the highway, protected against the worst excesses of the offshore winds. The beach, with a sandy spit that forms a shallow cove for swimmers, is dotted by rocks that make good points from which to fish the outer shore.

**Lincoln Beach,** just north of the park, begins a long string of beach towns, some of them given over to cottage owners, others of them mainly designed for tourists. The beaches are, consistently, wide and sandy. Most of them course along below sheer-faced bluffs of sandstone.

**Gleneden Beach** adjoins Lincoln Beach, and like it has a wide sandy beach on the seaward side of a row of motels and resort cottages.

**Taft,** around on the north shore Siletz Bay, is the south end of 10 miles of resort beach. Siletz Bay is a most irregular body of water, its sandy shoreline tacking back and forth in a seemingly endless series of spits and coves. The bay itself is dotted with sandbars as a further complication for boaters. All of this only improves the quality of the bay as a fishing and crabbing center. Taft and the smaller, middle-bay towns of Cutler City and Kernville offer excellent facilities for salmon and flounder fishing, and for ring-crabbing.

In this bay, the main run of Chinooks begins in August and peaks in September. The silvers start coming in during September and run strongly through October and into November.

**Nelscott,** adjoining Taft just outside the bay mouth, resumes the sandy strand begun at Lincoln Beach. The gently sloping beach is safe enough so children can frolic in the surf when the sea is at all calm.

**Delake,** a resort town, spreads out on the ocean side of U.S. 101, and east of it along one shore of Devil's Lake, a five-mile-long body of water much used by hydroplaners and other boat racers.

**Oceanlake** just to the north, has most of the lakeshore piers as well as a broad sandy beach below a bluff. It is a village single-mindedly organized to give tourists places to stay and entertainments to pursue.

**Devils Lake State Park,** between the two towns, has two faces. On the lake side it is developed for swimming, picnicking, and camping. The ocean side is broad sandy beach left in its original state for the ideal enjoyment of sun bathers and beachwalkers. A natural curiosity connects the two parts. It is the "D" River, advertised as the world's shortest. It courses a few more than 400 yards from Devil's Lake to its debouchement in the Pacific Ocean.

A recent reincorporation lumped all of the towns from Cutler City to Oceanlake into one new city, Lincoln City. But the district names survive.

**Roads End** a small, grey-weathered community of resort cottages and summer homes contrasts with the rather gaudier towns south along the highway. It fronts on a gravelly beach reached by a spur road that winds two miles northwest from its junction with U.S. 101 at the north edge of Lincoln City. The agate hunting is good, and this beach collects more drift in general than those to the south.

It is the north fringe of the Twenty Miracle Miles, which stretch very close to thirty taken altogether.

**Wecoma Beach,** a cheerful resort town, is at the junction of U.S. 101 and the road to Roads End.

# Historic northwest quarter

The Columbia River in a fine show of political impartiality deposits its cargo of Washington basalt sand in equal amounts on either side of its wide mouth. The northwest corner of Oregon benefits from this as much as Washington does, but uses the result rather differently than does the adjoining state.

There is nowhere near as much industry in this corner as there is in neighboring southwest Washington, partly because there is less harbor and no opportunity at all for oysters. The industrial part of north coast Oregon is Tillamook County, where the industry is cheese. The wide plain along the river mouth is given over almost entirely to resort activity.

Razor clams attract far the greatest number of shore users to the resorts. Swimming is important, too, on some good protected beaches. Not far south of the river mouth Tillamook Head is the first of several outcrops that make rocky homes for tidepool animals and good territory for skin divers. Tillamook County is indented by several small bays that add other-than-razor clams and crabs to the range of shore activity. Tillamook and Astoria are among the ports for sportfishing vessels, and surf fishing is productive all along.

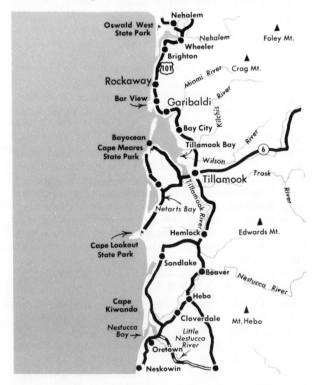

**SHORESIDE CAMPING:** *Whalen Island County Park (Sand Lake) (40 units); Cape Lookout State Park (194 units, 53 trailer units); Barview County Park (125 units, 39 trailer units); Oswald West State Park (21 units).*
**SHORESIDE ACCOMMODATIONS:** *Neskowin, Pacific City, Oceanside-Netarts, Garibaldi, Rockaway, Manzanita, Nehalem. Inshore motels at Tillamook. Write Tillamook County C of C, 2105 First Street, Tillamook for list.*

Driftwood stacks up along these shores, and all kinds of drift is to be found mixed in with the wood, starting with Japanese fishing floats. In fact, this is one of the few areas where historic bits and pieces can be turned up with a little effort, and historic treasures are at least to be hoped for. Spanish vessels and English ones that have gone down over the span of two centuries have left fittings, beeswax, and even silver goblets for others to find.

## Tillamook County

A long, skinny county, Tillamook is famous mainly for cheddar cheese of distinct character. Its neighboring counties north and south have out-publicized it in matters concerning the sea and its shore. In those counties, U.S. 101 sticks to the shore with tenacity. In Tillamook County, the federal highway wanders inshore several miles and stays there except for a stretch north of Tillamook Bay.

This, for beachcombers, is a happy state of affairs. It leaves a considerable amount of sideroad exploring to be done.

### THE SOUTHWEST CORNER

Compared to the neighboring area to the south, the southwest corner of Tillamook County is plain and sober. Vacationers often find the modesty becoming.

**Neskowin,** on the sea at the south border of the county, attracts families in numbers to a broad sandy beach that is somewhat protected from heavy surf by Proposal Rock just offshore. A golf course ambles along the back side of the beach, and mounts a sandy hill, giving beachcombers with golf clubs an excuse to go up there for the view. Sun-warmed creek waters fill a summer lagoon in the backshore, making a safe swimming and wading hole for children. Fishing in the surf is for sea perch, sea trout, and flounder.

Between Neskowin and the town of Tillamook, U.S. 101 rolls along in cheerfully pastoral country, uphill and down, and never in a fashion to suit hurriers. The distance is 32 miles. After Neskowin, the shore is never in sight.

**Pacific City** is known to those who know it all as the Home of the Dory Fleet.

The dory is hardly a plentiful vessel on this coast. Flat bottomed, with flaring sides, common in New England ports and really at home among cod-fishing Newfoundlanders, it nonetheless serves best of all small boats in this wave-buffeted bay, where sports fishermen go bravely out to sea to fish for salmon from them.

The dories troll, once offshore, under the power of outboard motors. But the trip through the surf is strictly an oarsman's game. The launching point is at the north side of Pacific City in the lee of Cape Kiwanda, with further protection from Haystack Rock offshore. Even with that, novices go green at the gills as often as not while the boats pitch and roll through the line of breakers.

The prime quarry is salmon—Chinook or silvers from late June until the end of September—just offshore or south a mile or so off the mouth of the Nestucca. It costs a mini-

*Driftwood frames fisherman on Tillamook Spit. Outbound dory at Pacific City*

mum of $10 a day, so early limiters or blanked fishermen get extra enjoyment out of good bottom fishing for cod and halibut around Haystack Rock and off a nearby reef.

Every year in mid-July the two-day Dory Derby pays skill and persistence with prizes. Win or lose, this derby is unique on a coast that has several score salmon derbies every year. Told properly, the adventure story of any dory expedition should not wear the grandchildren out for years. Reservations are always in order, and can be obtained by writing Dutch Shermer's Sporting Goods, Pacific City.

Pacific City has other charms. Nestucca Bay Spit south of Cape Kiwanda curves long, its sandy beach wide below a 10-foot bluff crowned with summer cottages. Driftwood collects on it in immense quantities each winter during the storms. Public parking lots are at the county launching ramp at the base of Cape Kiwanda, and at the end of the main road into town, about at the mid-point of the beach.

The same waves that make dory launching an enterprise of considerable instability also serve to get surfboard pilots up and riding in the opposite direction. Oregon has only a few beaches with suitable surf. This one, although it poses no challenge to experts, does well enough for novices and intermediates.

Finally, skin-diving around the cape will reward a diver with a fair harvest of scallops among other edible and inedible animals.

Pacific City is on a loop road of some loveliness. The south leg, which joins U.S. 101 three miles north of Neskowin, winds along the bank of the Little Nestucca River under a canopy of alders. The north leg follows the lush valley of the (big) Nestucca River, intersecting with U.S. 101 at Cloverdale. A still longer north leg goes past other beaches.

**Tierra del Mar,** first beach on the extension of the loop, has a county park on a wide beach as sandy as Pacific City's, but more exposed to surf. From Pacific City, follow small road signs for "Sand Lake".

**Sand Lake,** another several miles north, is in fact a small bay. A county park on its east shore (Whalen Island County Park) gives access to a sandy swimming beach. There are some flounder and crabs in the shallows, too. The park has good picnic facilities. Around on the west side of the bay a forest service campground and picnic park gives access to a bay beach and the ocean shore as well. A spur road leads around the bay's north end to this park (Sand Beach Park). North of the community of Sand Lake, the county road turns east to a junction with U.S. 101 at the town of Hemlock, 13 miles south of Tillamook.

Cape Lookout sits in plain view only four miles up the beach from Sand Beach Park, but no road connects the two areas. Motorists have to go to Tillamook, then loop back to the southwest on another road.

## CAPE MEARES AND CAPE LOOKOUT

It takes a day to make all the stops from Tillamook out to Cape Meares, then downcoast to Cape Lookout State Park. To get full value from each of the stops would take more like a week to 10 days. On a coast where scenery usually unfolds for miles at a time, this section tends to reveal itself by feet and inches.

Tillamook Bay south spit stretches for miles, until it almost closes the bay mouth. The effect is intentional, and is reinforced by a breakwater at the base of the spit. The paved Bay Front Road runs alongside the bay (follow signs for Cape Meares from downtown Tillamook) to the base of the spit. From there, a rough, split-level gravel road goes out to the end of the breakwater. The low half is one-way outbound; the high half is for the return trip.

On the bay side, clammers can dig for gapers, cockles, and littlenecks from the parking area at the north end of the road all the way to the tip of the spit, known as Pitcher Point. On the ocean side, five miles of steep-faced beach collect enormous amounts of drift. In the sandy spots, a few razor clams lurk, mainly due west of the breakwater.

Aside from the access across sand dunes west of the parking lot there is another point where a spur of the main Cape Meares Road comes close to the beach. The spur goes straight at the fork where signs point south for Cape Meares. No formal parking exists on the backside of a steep mound of rock and enormous driftwood. Visitors just stop and walk over the top, to be confronted by a long strand of giant surrealistic driftwood and a length of shoreline where the surf fishing can be highly productive.

**Cape Meares State Park,** on a wooded headland just south of the spit, offers no beach access. It offers instead an ancient lighthouse, and a picnic area with fine views out to sea and downcoast. The bay road, after it loops west and then south, climbs the headland. Near the crest a faintly marked access road leads down to the light station and a ten-car parking area.

**Short Beach,** a mile long at low tide, lies just south of Cape Meares. It has a good supply of collectable driftwood most of the year, and agates mix with other stones along the beach. At the south end, elevated tidepools contain colonies of sea anemones and starfish, and rock oysters are to be had for sturdy sea stews from some of the softer rocks along the outcrop that closes the beach to further progress south. At the north end, a somewhat similar series of tidepools and a lacy waterfall please both eye and ear.

Beyond the tidepools at the south end, Lost Boy Cave beckons to adventurous spirits. It once beckoned too well to a small boy, according to local legend, whose fate gave the cave a name. In these times full of forethought, further misadventure was ruled out by the addition of an escape shaft at the rear of the cave, but it still pays to keep an eye on the tide.

The trail from the Cape Meares Road down to the beach is not marked. It begins near the bottom of the grade south of Cape Meares State Park, near a roadside culvert.

**Oceanside,** a small resort community graced by some outstanding examples of vacation home architecture of this and a couple of earlier periods, nestles comfortably at the base of the same headland that is visible from Short Beach. A wide beach of clean sand shoals gently and without bars or other current-producing underwater topography. The water is cold, but entirely safe for swimmers. Surf fishing along the beach is good. At the north, a tongue of rock sticks out into the surf. On it, dimly visible, a painted sign warns that no one should attempt to round the point. Enough people tried and lost to cause the blasting of a short, stand-up tunnel through the rock. The tunnel emerges on the other side into a rocky cove full of offshore rocks, fine tidepools, and agate-bearing gravel. It also brings a nature-oriented beachcomber as close as he can get to Three Arch Rocks National Bird and Sea Lion Refuge, a cluster of monoliths a few hundred yards out from shore. On a lucky day, a visitor will find himself at ringside for a free-lance sea lion act. The pups seem to enjoy extemporizing in the surf with or without human audiences.

The unwary can get caught by an incoming tide beyond a series of low rocky points two hundred yards north of the tunnel. The same rocks can be rounded easily at low tide.

A public parking area adjoins the main beach at the north end of the Oceanside business street running north from the Cape Meares Loop Road.

**Netarts,** down the track two miles from Oceanside, exists mainly as a boat launching area. The new buildings of the village perch on a headland above the jetty of Netarts Bay. Charter boats go over the bar for salmon from the small harbor at the inland end of the north jetty.

In the bay itself, crabbing is concentrated along the east side, in channels from Netarts south to Whiskey Creek.

Clams tend to be mainly on the inshore side of the spit, which points north from Cape Lookout State Park. The beds are reached most easily by boat from the ramp at Netarts.

From Netarts, one road heads toward Tillamook, and another continues south to Cape Lookout State Park, at the south tip of Netarts Bay.

**Cape Lookout State Park** occupies both the spit enclosing Netarts Bay and the bold headland thrusting out from the shore to the south. It is a big park, and a popular one. The size of its parking lot attests to that.

Along the ocean side of the spit, a broad and clean beach slopes gently into the surf. On its sandy surface, sand dollar shells wash up with each high tide, and in winter enough sand washes out to sea to expose sizable gravel beds. These last contain enough agates to keep collectors coming back. Rockhounds and geologists enjoy the cape more, though, for the presence of extensive flows of pillow lava along the headland, a two-mile long spur of igneous rock that stemmed entirely from a gigantic lava flow. The pillows are at the base, formed when molten lava coursed into the sea and cooled rapidly.

Tidepools and viewpoints as well as lava pillows are at the ends of a plethora of pleasant walking trails, which course along in the duff from thick stands of Sitka spruce.

Fine picnic sites are close to the parking area. A two-acre picnic park donated by Crown-Zellerbach Corp. augments the state park facilities. It is on the south tip of Netarts Bay a few hundred yards east of the state park entrance.

## RESORTS AND LEGENDS

On the north side of Tillamook Bay, US.. 101 comes close to the shore on its route through a string of towns oriented in this era toward beach visitors, but with roots that go back to a most mysterious, Iberian moment of history. There is, in addition to good fishing, surf swimming, and rockhounding, some opportunity to poke about in search of ancient and legendary Spanish treasure.

**Garibaldi,** a mill town and fishing harbor near the north

# Winter's visitors, the shorebirds

**Curlew with Godwits**

**Long-billed dowitchers**

*Avocet*

*Willets*

*Killdeer*

The shorebirds are smaller than the ducks and geese of the Pacific Flyway, but they travel farther every year. At least half of the 40 species that winter between San Diego and Cape Flattery can be seen commonly at any point on the coast where a sand spit, bay margin, marsh, or slough offers sustenance from fall through spring.

A good pair of binoculars is the best way to watch the seven most commonly seen of these birds or any of their peers which leave these balmy shores to summer above the Arctic Circle.

Sandpipers are the best known of the shorebirds, and were even before movies were invented. Western and least sandpipers fly together, in flocks as numerous as 1,000 birds. The flocks wheel, land, and fly away on signals only they know. The western is the larger of the two birds, has a heavier bill and dark legs. The least has yellow legs. Both have thickly spotted breasts.

Killdeers are also small shorebirds, seen both in water and inland. The name is the onomatopoeia of their call.

Watchers who happen on a nesting place are treated to a superb bit of acting. An adult will limpingly whimper away from the nest, dragging a wing; and keeping just a hop ahead of a pursuer. When the bird is satisfied that the danger over, it will leap into the air and streak for home. Dogs and wild predators are notoriously gullible.

Curlews are the largest brown birds of the shore. Two species, the Hudsonian and the long-billed curlew, appear in small flocks. The long-bill, as its name implies, has a very long bill that curves downward. The mottled brown birds with bill curved upward are marbled godwits. They are seen more frequently than curlews, and often travel in the company of willets.

Dowitchers are smaller than curlews, godwits, and willets. They have long straight bills, and a dark line crossing each eye. They are often seen with curlews and plovers.

Willets are easily identified by their black and white wing markings, and in flight they make a distinctive *whee-wee-wee* sound.

Avocets are among the handsomest shorebirds. Their backs are boldly striped with black and white, their undersides are white, and their legs and upturned bills are bright blue. With the appearance of spring plumage, their black heads change to cinnamon.

Plovers are closely related to killdeers, but have only one neck stripe, and assume a short, squatty stance.

A good field manual: *A Field Guide to Western Birds* by Roger Tory Peterson (Houghton-Mifflin, 1961, $4.95).

*On a warm summer day, Short Sands is a beautiful beach for walkers*

jetty of the bay, has a Coast Guard station that should be on recruiting posters and a flock of rental and charter boats that will take sports fishermen either to the northeastern arc of the bay after flatfish, into the jetty mouth for salmon in season and rockfish anytime, or out over the bar for deep-sea trolling.

One length of pier in the fishing harbor is given over to a trim, black-hulled schooner, a two-master called the Morning Star II. She is 40 feet overall, a precise duplicate of the original, which served the Tillamook coast communities from 1855 to 1860 when no roads connected them to the interior.

Built in 1959 as an observance of the Oregon Statehood Centennial, the vessel sailed under her own canvas to Portland, a voyage that took her along the route of her forebear and that recalled how powerful the sea was as a connecting agent in the histories and economies of the towns along the Oregon shore.

The original *Morning Star* acquired all her fittings from the bones of the U.S. Navy survey schooner *Shark*, which went aground and broke up on the Columbia bar in September of 1846. A party of volunteers travelled overland eight years later to get the metalwork and haul it back to Tillamook Bay.

The rest of the *Shark* is spread around the north coast. Cannon Beach is named for a cannon taken from the vessel, which cannon is mounted by the side of the road near that town along with a capstan bar and a suitably informative plaque. In Astoria, Shark Rock commemorates the unhappy visit of the vessel to the area. The residents of the region were not sure whether to cast their lot with the British or with the United States, and the presence of the naval vessel disquieted most of the settlers.

Her sinking was viewed with relief by all save the crew.

**Barview County Park,** its access road just outside the bay mouth, offers an unusually close look at the whole idea of jetties, and further provides good rock fishing and skin-diving from the jetty and good surf fishing farther upshore.

The park is a large one, with picnic facilities as an added amenity. Most of it is devoted to campsites, but it has a long sandy beach for day use in addition to the several access points to the jetty itself. The effects of such structures on harbor bars and surf zones in general can be observed clearly at this park, and from comfortably pleasant surroundings.

**Rockaway,** just more than three miles north, is the largest of several beach towns between Barview and the mouth of Nehalem Bay. Some of her highway businesses have fallen on hard times, so her skirts look a bit tattered. But if the old girl can't play the romantic lead, she does a fine job with a character role. The modern resorts three blocks west of the highway look out over a magnificently wide and clean beach, safe for swimming and a pleasure to stroll along in quest of drift. The town makes a good headquarters point for trips north to Nehalem Bay and south to Cape Meares, Cape Lookout, and way points.

**Nehalem** and **Manzanita** between them hold the key to the local treasure mystery. Somehow, a considerable amount of Spanish beeswax got buried in the beach sand on the ocean side of Nehalem Sandspit. Indians and early settlers used it in local commerce during the early 1800's. Sizable chunks of it kept turning up through the 1930's. Beachcombers still find an occasional small piece in the sands after winter storms.

Samples have been dated accurately as being of late 1600's manufacture.

How and when it got there remains a matter of some conjecture, but the popular theory is that the Spanish galleon *San Francisco Xavier* was blown northeast of her intended course from Manila to Mexico by a storm, and grounded on Nehalem Spit. Some local Indian legends lend credence to this idea. Spanish maritime registers list the *San Francisco Xavier* as having gone missing in 1705, a logical date for explaining the riddle. The remains of a ship of galleon-like lines poked up through storm-thinned sands off and on again for years on end from the mid-1800's until as late as 1930.

One Indian legend also recounts how the crew took a heavy chest from a mystery ship, and carried it up to a spot on Neah-Kah-Nie Mountain, burying it there with a body draped across the top to ward off would-be robbers. The mountain is pock-marked with hundreds of holes dug by local and imported treasure hunters, none of whom has succeeded to this point.

It is a good chance to participate in a classic legend when more routine pursuits pall. Nehalem Bay and the ocean shore outside it have good fishing, good clamming, and good beachcombing for driftwood, glass fishing floats and other typical drift. **Nehalem Bay State Park,** only lightly developed, covers most of the spit. Access is through Manzanita, two miles west of U.S. 101, as is a marked access road to Neah-Kah-Nie beach, northwest of the town.

**Oswald West State Park** occupies the last miles of the Tillamook County coastline. It is a succession of lofty turnout points on the west shoulder of Mount Neah-Kah-Nie, and an intervening series of attractive beaches.

A roadside parking area marked by signs reading Short Sand Beach gives access to a pleasant place for idle strolling, sun-bathing, informal picnicking, and similarly relaxed pursuits. The hardest part is the trail from the parking lot to the shore, and it isn't very. Farther north, Falcon Cove or Smuggler's Cove are other beaches easily explored after a short hike down a trail connecting roadside parking lot to beach. Falcon Cove has an extensive pile of driftwood on it. A picnic-and-camping area lies on the east side of the highway, between Short Sand and Falcon Cove beaches.

Arch Rock Cape, the county line, is just to the north.

# The North Corner

Being adjacent to the mouth of a great river, the most northerly section of the Oregon Coast has a great legacy of historic explorations and maritime adventure. Its greatest charm is that the historic character of the place exists side by side with carnival resorts and a thriving center for conventions, a different atmosphere than neighboring Tillamook County exudes.

### CANNON BEACH AND ECOLA

An only slightly different mood sets in north of Tillamook County through the highway tunnel through Arch Rock Cape. The coast of Clatsop county attends strictly to tourism; it has no other function. Still, the first miles of it are relatively subdued.

**Tolovana Park,** the first community north of the cape, has few commercial resorts compared to Cannon Beach. It is mainly a colony of summer homes placed to take advantage of the wide beach of basaltic sand with its crop of razor clams, the last really sizeable beds south of the Columbia River mouth.

The sand stretches unbroken for seven miles, ending just north beyond Cannon Beach. Some driftwood around Arch Rock Cape is virtually the only year around litter on it.

**Cannon Beach** has a main street typical of resort beach main streets, the admixture of the fundamental grocery, drug store and service station with purely diversionary curio shop, hotdoggery, and allied enterprises. West of this street, cottages and motels line streets that end along the back beach.

Pocketed between Arch Rock Cape on the south and Tillamook Head on the north, this broad beach can be used for surf swimming (on the incoming tide only), surf fishing, razor clam digging, and, after a suitable walk, tidepool exploring along the capes. The activities are overt, well-advertised, and the equals of their reputations. They take place in a remarkably handsome scenic landscape. Hills heavily forested with Sitka spruce tower in a ring behind the beach. Offshore, Haystack Rock adds its gloomily handsome bulk to an already rocky shore. (This is the real Haystack Rock. Every portly monolith along this coast goes by the name, but this is the one in promotion literature photographs.) Inexperienced climbers can walk out to it at low tide and clamber up. But they cannot get back down unless they fall or are rescued by the Coast Guard. The Coast Guard, as a result, strongly counsels against climbing onto the rock.

**Ecola State Park,** on the south half of Tillamook Head, defies extensive civilization. Its terrain seldom comes even close to level, with the result that its magnificently craggy shoreline creates a genuine sense of adventure in the few people who persevere in walking its historic trails, and in poking about its secluded coves.

A paved but narrow road forks west from the access road to Cannon Beach and climbs snakily up to a tabled bluff overlooking the town to the south. This is the developed part of the park, with picnic sites, gas stoves, paved trails leading to a series of dramatic overlooks. The road continues north to two other overlooks and picnic sites of lesser size but equal quality.

Faint along the intervening bluffs is a trail from Elk Creek just south of the park to Seaside. It follows the approximate route of the party Captain William Clark led from Fort Clatsop to the carcass of the whale the party discovered in 1806. All told, the park extends along six and-one-half miles of seashore. Two sandy beaches are at the south edge. A steep cove on the north side of Ecola Point (the main picnic area) has fine rock fishing. From there north, along Indian Beach and Indian Point (another picnic area), the shore has good tidepools, and a fair surfing area at one end of Indian Beach. Still farther north is Tillamook Head, the most northerly of the picnic areas and the best viewpoint for looking out to the abandoned Tillamook Light, more than a mile out at sea.

This light in its operating days withstood the violent

*Wooded picnic* site at Ecola. The dwindling remains of the Peter Iredale

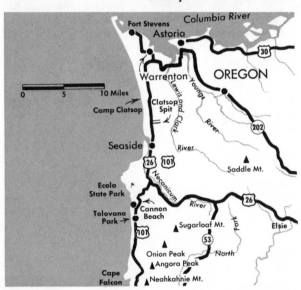

*SHORESIDE CAMPING: Fort Stevens State Park ( 259 units, 226 trailer units). SHORESIDE ACCOMMODA-TIONS: Cannon Beach, Seaside-Gearhart. Write Seaside-Gearhart C of C, 20 N. Columbia, Seaside, for list. Inshore motels and hotels in Astoria. No list available.*

*Early outpost at Astoria is a fishing village now*

assaults of a stormy Pacific for winter after winter, but not without scars. Its worst moment came during a December storm in which a wave-propelled boulder arched above the light, 139 feet above the sea, and fell through the roof. It weighed 135 pounds and made a noticeable hole. Lesser rocks broke the windows around the lantern on several occasions, and also clogged the throat of the foghorn. One keeper reported that a solid sea descended on the roof of the tower during a storm in 1902. It is no wonder that Coast Guard lighthouse crews were grateful for the development of automatic beacons and loran. At all events, Tillamook Light is no more.

## SEASIDE, CARNIVAL TOWN

This is the carnival town of the northwest coast, the counterpart to Santa Cruz in California's northerly latitudes, or Santa Monica in Los Angeles county. The two-mile beach of sand is backed by a paved beachwalk that would look just as much at home at Cannes, or Brighton in England, or anywhere else huge crowds gather to enjoy ocean swimming, long strolls, and the patented pleasures of fun houses, ferris wheels, and cotton candy.

**Seaside,** largely described in the preceding  paragraph,

gets year-round play from Portlanders and college kids from all directions. They come on weekends and whenever else they can. In summer, it is a fine family resort because the beach is patrolled by platoons of lifeguards and because it has hundreds of diversions for youngsters, ranging from good clamming and surf bathing right on down the carnival street, and on to golf courses and lakeside parks a mile or two back from the shore.

**Gearhart,** its beach separated from Seaside's by the mouth of the Necanicum River, is advertised as Oregon's convention capitol. It is. Its entertainments are, even more than Seaside's, divided between the outdoors during the day and the indoors at night. From here, the wide, sandy beach extends straight north 23 miles to the mouth of the Columbia. A walk north out of town on the salty edge of the Clatsop plain will produce a sudden change from the cheerfully brassy atmosphere of the resort to a splendidly lonely, wind-swept existence on the edge of a changeable sea. A man willing to walk far enough will, sooner or later, leave behind everything but razor clams, crabs, and beach grass. If he keeps going beyond that point he will regain the company of man at Fort Stevens State Park.

## AN HISTORIC PLAIN

The Columbia River is one of America's great rivers, the essential of the opening of the Northwest Territories to colonization, the connecting tissue of the regional commerce, the wellspring of industrial power. It is only natural that its mouth should be the site of a substantial amount of history.

The Lewis and Clark expedition arrived on the mouth of the river in 1805, and stayed through the winter of 1806. Sea captains had been there earlier, but it was the expedition that started the push of Americans and British alike into the new territory.

**Fort Clatsop,** on the Lewis and Clark River that pours into Youngs Bay west of Astoria, is a reconstitution of the Lewis and Clark camp and a national monument. Its low log buildings can be reached either from Seaside-Gearhart, or from Astoria. In it is the best place to get started on a tour of the significant history of the region.

**Fort Stevens State Park,** eight miles north of Fort Clatsop and 13 miles west of Astoria on a spur road off U.S. 101, marks the site of a fort that came later than Clatsop. Clatsop was a tentative probe. Stevens was a matter of American control of the river mouth. It was built in 1864 to keep Confederate gunboats out of the Columbia, and was intermittently active through the end of World War II, to guard against all comers. As affairs turned out, no firing took place in the neighborhood until 1942, when a Japanese submarine lobbed a few shells over the hulk of the *Peter Iredale*, and by then the fort was in no position to fire back.

They were the only enemy shells which struck the United States in the course of World War II, and they killed nothing more than some beach grass near the old artillery emplacements of Battery Russell.

The park activities center on some small lakes trapped in the dunes a mile and more inshore, where the water is warm and quiet for swimming, and picnic facilities ring sandy lake shores.

The ocean front is, like all of this coast, an immensely wide strip of fine basaltic sand. Razor clams are abundant wherever the surf beats in unhampered, and when the morning tide ebbs across the troughs between sand bars, there are always a few crabs cut off from escape to the sea.

Surf fishing is good. Spur roads lead out through the old fort (which is well north of the park headquarters) to the jetty, which also has good fishing.

In the mid-section of the park's ocean beach, just across the sand from a large parking lot, embedded in the surf zone as it has been since 1906, is the hull of the *Peter Iredale*, or at least what is left of it. It made a photogenic wreck from the day it went ashore, and became in time something of a trademark for this area.

She was British registry, 278 feet overall, with steel plates on iron frames, and she was inbound under the command of Captain H. Lawrence on the night of October 24. The captain decided to stand off the river mouth and wait for a pilot. A heavy southwest wind was making up, and it seemed better to shorten sail and wait rather than run for it. During the night, somehow she got into the surf, and was dismasted. All hands were gotten off by the lifesaving crew from Point Adams, but there was no refloating the ship.

That is the romantic half of the story. The other half is that sailors had to be crimped (Shanghaied if it is more pleasing) to get crews for her, and the unlucky who served aboard the vessel called her "the slow coach." She was, to give some idea, 28 days out of Salina Cruz, Mexico, when she hove to off the river mouth.

Bulky tub or no, she made a very fine looking shipwreck and an astonishingly durable one. Her famous bowsprit didn't carry away until a storm in 1963. Her last duty was in the war years, when she was the anchoring point for barbed wire the Army strung all over the place after the incident of the submarine.

**Astoria,** the present day center of Clatsop county business and legal affairs, is a lumber port, a fishing village, the departure point of the bridge across the Columbia river to Washington State, and a city filled with museums.

The maritime history of the coast, the Columbia River bar, and the river itself is neatly wrapped up in an old frame building at 16th and Exchange Streets, just a couple of blocks up the hill from the old Astoria-Megler ferry pier. There charts, models, fittings, logbooks and guides with great local knowledge can tell the story complete and well.

A blockhouse from Fort Astoria, the original fur-trading post of the region, occupies a corner between 14th and 15th on Exchange Street. (Exchange runs east and west; the numbered streets go north and south.)

The old Flavel Mansion, a wonder of carpenter's Gothic, is on the west side of the business district, on 8th between Exchange and Duane Streets. In it, the Clatsop County Historical Museum tells all the stories skipped by the other two museums, and the two Forts.

**Warrenton,** a town built around its small boat harbor 13 miles west of Astoria, adjoins Fort Stevens. Charter boats from it go out the south channel and across the Columbia River bar after salmon from June until the end of September.

# WASHINGTON COAST

# Sandy southwest coast

Washington's southwest quarter owes much of its economic existence to the sea. Its commerce depends heavily on deepwater ports in the Columbia River, or on its two broad bays. A considerable part of the traffic has to do with saltwater edibles caught or raised in the vicinity, these being salmon, oysters, and razor clams.

Vacationers in the area come mainly to fish for salmon or dig for razor clams, and their sharing of space with professionals tends to affect the nature of the resorts.

The theme is understatement. The buildings are mainly sturdy cottages built to withstand howling sea winds in winter, and to comfortably house tired, cold, wet people back from a fishing or a clamming trip, or a walk through a winter storm in search of drift.

If the buildings are subdued, so is the physical appearance of the countryside. The ocean beaches are broad expanses of sand backed by low, grassy dunes. The hills inshore are gentle and repetitious in outline.

It is a place for people who want to do something with the outdoors other than admire it from afar.

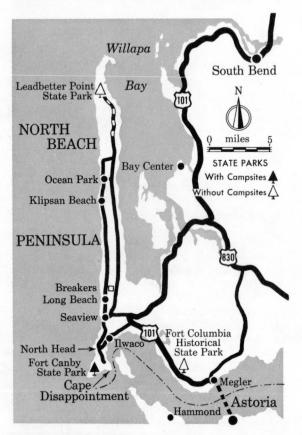

**SHORESIDE CAMPING:** *Fort Canby State Park (west of Ilwaco) (60 units); Bush-Pacific Pioneer State Park (12 miles so. of South Bend) (12 units).* **SHORESIDE ACCOMMODATIONS:** *All along Long Beach Peninsula. Write Peninsula Resort Association, P.O. Box 6, Long Beach, 98631, for list. Inshore accommodations at South Bend-Raymond. No list available.*

In summer, the coastal resorts are mobbed on any weekend of a minus tide, and heavily populated at any time at all. Reservations are required during the entire period of school vacations. The crowds remain substantial as long as the salmon fishing is good. Toward the end of September, a fair number of the resorts button up until spring. (Inland they stay open until later in the season because this is popular hunting country, too.)

## North Beach Peninsula

Except for North Head, which looms gloomily above the Columbia River north jetty, the North Beach Peninsula barely shows on a topographic map. It is a 28-mile-long spit of sand quarried out of a basaltic plateau in central Washington and carried down to the sea by the river, then washed back ashore by the sea. Hardly any part of it is more than 20 feet above sea level.

On the peninsula are some sizable cranberry bogs, several oyster fisheries, and a flock of resort towns.

### AT THE RIVER MOUTH

Lighthouses, salmon fishing, and jetty fishing occupy the attentions of most of the visitors to this most southwesterly corner of Washington.

**Ilwaco,** inside the river mouth by a narrow margin, is the only town of the region which is not devoted mainly to shellfish. It is devoted to swimming fish. Its 700-boat protected harbor is the home port of a fleet of commercial and charter vessels which cruises the river and offshore waters for salmon all summer long and until the last spawning schools pass upstream or the weather gets too vigorous.

The Columbia River bar, tamed as it has been by channels and jetties, still is no place to get caught when the weather makes up. In the long history of navigation across the bar, more than 2,000 ships have been lost or damaged at a cost of more than 1,500 lives. The surf on the outer bar runs at an average height of 20 feet in a winter storm, and the waves pounding ashore register on a seismograph some miles inland.

The Lewis and Clark expedition in the winter of 1805 got an early taste of how it is on a small boat during foul weather. The whole party was driven ashore on its first exposure to the river mouth for fear of swamping its canoes in turbulent waves. Lewis wrote in his Journal that ". . . . at two o'clock the flood tide set in, accompanied by a high wind from the south, which, about four o'clock, shifted to the southwest, and blew almost a gale directly from the sea. The immense waves now broke over the place where were encamped, and the large trees, some of them five or six feet thick, which had lodged at the point, were drifted over our camp. . . .We remained in the water and drenched with rain during the rest of the day."

Boats are better-made at present, but the winter weather is no great deal improved over last century's. Some of the memorabilia of this history (and some sunny moments, too) can be examined in the museum at **Fort Columbia**

*North Head Light* stands guard on grey, blustery winter day

just a few miles east of Ilwaco on U.S. 101, on the way to the bridge to Astoria, Oregon. In addition to its duties as a museum, the fort also has a state park swimming beach and picnic area. The grounds are a gently sloping hillside well blanketed by trees.

**Fort Canby State Park** occupies the lowland between Cape Disappointment and North Head, giving access to both of these and to the north jetty (Peacock Spit to old mariners).

Cape Disappointment, crowned by one of the most beautifully set lighthouses of the coast, is on the river side of the jetty, directly at its base. The tower stands out white against a black-green backdrop of wooded headland. Below, waves fight the river current, and break into spray against the rocks. Between the jetty's base and those rocks is a short crescent of smooth sand, named Waikiki Beach at a moment of excess zeal, but for all of that still a good swimming beach for youngsters in fair weather.

The road into the park splits into three just inside the gate. The south fork goes to the cape (visits to the light by appointment with the district Coast Guard commander only), the north one into the park camping area, and the middle choice is the jetty road. It is an unusually primitive affair that jounces and bumps for more than a mile in the lee of the towering mound of rip-rap to a parking area adjacent to the best fishing spot on the jetty. There is almost inevitably a crowd of warmly dressed men and women wedged against the boulders and waiting for fish to strike.

This is one of the fine vantage points in all the world for winter storm watching. The bar is a seething mass of waves, and there is plenty of spray flying up from the jetty. Off to the north, waves beat against the rocks of North Head, and in between a sandy beach takes the long rollers full on. For sheer variety of wave action, it is an uncommonly compact spectacle.

To get to Fort Canby from Ilwaco, go west at the lone signal-controlled intersection on U.S. 101. No sign is visible to motorists approaching from Megler, and the road does not look promising at that point, but it gets there. From points on the peninsula, take Holman Road west in Seaview, and follow it south as it becomes Willow Road .

**North Head** comes into view before the park on the latter road, which joins the road from Ilwaco just outside the park gate. The light station can be visited from 1 to 3 p.m. daily in summer and weekends the year around. Its bluff is a fine viewpoint for a look back up the peninsula, across the river, or out to sea. There is some rock fishing in the coves on the north side of it, and hiking trails run helter-skelter around it. A private campground occupies the inner curve, called Beard's Hollow, of the cove.

# It takes fast digging to catch razor clams

*Razor clam prospector seeks prey with shovel*

*Once clam is located quick digging is required*

*A fine mess of clams rewards persistent digger*

In the Pacific Northwest it is an article of faith that the razor clam is the world's greatest clam. The matter of taste is individual, but there is no denying that this is the world's champion digger among clams."

An unofficial spokesman for the clammers themselves says that "digging for razor clams satisfies a man's basic urges to hunt, fish, and farm all in one gloriously difficult operation.

The cold statistics are these. Razor clams can dig at a steady rate of as much as nine inches a minute, to a depth of three feet or more. They live near the lower extreme of the tidal zone, with the hinged side of their long, slim shells faced out to sea. They inhabit only beaches where the surf sweeps in unchecked by offshore islands or other protection. The best concentrations for diggers seem to be on sand bars that retain an inch-deep glaze of water on the lowest tides of the year.

The animals seem to prefer the basalt sands washed out to sea by the Columbia River above all others. Washington's greatest concentrations occur along the sweep of shore from the river mouth north as far as Pacific Beach. Lesser numbers inhabit beaches at Moclips and Kalaloch, north of the Quinault Indian reservation. On the Oregon side, Seaside, Gearhart, and Cannon Beach are favored. A few beds occur farther south at Rockaway, Bayocean, and Netarts Bay Spit, but they are not extensive. In California, Humboldt Bay spit has some razors.

No amount of industry will catch up with a plummeting razor unless it is accompanied by some skill. A new hand with some instruction can score about 50% of the time. A tyro on his own may go home skunked.

A clam gun, for the uninitiated, is a shovel with a blade that is long and thin, like the clam is, and tilted at about a 20° angle. The guns can be bought or rented at curio shops, bus depots, doughnut stands, and everyplace else in the major beach areas near the Columbia River. They are provided free to the patrons of some resorts.

The professional technique, which takes practice, calls for working in the wash area of the waves, in an inch or more of water. The digger, after spotting the tip of a clam's siphon, shoves the clam gun in the sand six inches on the seaward side of the hole, and pushes the handle away seaward. The pressure thus exerted keeps the clam from burrowing. The digger then reaches in alongside the shovel blade, pulls the shovel out, and gropes for the quarry, which he wiggles back and forth like a loose tooth to break the suction.

Dry digging is easier for beginners, who are less apt to keep a wary eye on the surf, and not as apt to recognize the dime-sized dimple of the clam's siphon in the ebb and flow of water.

Dry diggers walk along just above the wave line, looking for a small circular depression in the packed sand. When one is spotted, the digger takes a quick shovelful of sand from the seaward side of the hole, lifting the sand straight up to avoid severing the clam's neck. Then he drops to his knees and digs with both hands, straight down. (Two-man teams do better, with one on shovel and the other kneeling, ready to dig.)

A net that can be fastened to the belt is the best way to carry clams. Gulls are expert bandits, and know how to get clams out of untended buckets.

Washington's daily bag limit is the first 18 clams dug. Oregon's is the first 24. Check Washington seasons.

*Sandy expanses* of Leadbetter Park invite explorers

*Fort Columbia* stands as reminder of pioneer days

## THE LONG, STRAIGHT SHORE

Several concentrations of resorts share the ocean beach of the peninsula.

**Long Beach** is the major town among three strung out along the seaward side of a peninsula that is variously called North Beach Peninsula and Long Beach Peninsula. **Seaview** is on its south flank and **Ocean Park** is several miles to the north of it. The three resemble each other. The main road through each is lined with resorts, curio shops, small restaurants and the omnipresent service stations. Each town has one road or two leading west to the edge of the beach where wooden arches or metal ones invite visitors to drive out onto the sand and head up or down the surf line at prudent speed and above the clam beds. (It is illegal to drive on them).

It is possible to drive 28 miles thus, at the price of encrusting the underside of an automobile with salt. It is the longest drive of its kind in the world, at least among countries where there are automobiles. It is handy for clammers, who otherwise might be faced with very long walks to favored beds.

The few public accesses are augmented by dozens of paths from private resorts.

Most of the resorts these days are 500 yards or more from the edge of the water, a result of episodic extensions of the river jetties, Every time the jetties have been extended, the shore currents have moved a corresponding distance west, and have dumped their loads of sand a bit sooner than they did before.

There is a hummocky ridge running the length of all these towns. It was the back edge of the beach as late as World War I when big shoreside hotels were all the rage.

The patina of age that softens the area is one of its principal charms. Very few buildings on the peninsula are of the concrete block era. Chrome and neon intrude but little. Weathered frame structures and painted board signs predominate. Fresh paint does not endure well the corrosive effect of wind and winter rain, but it shows up every spring anyway.

In summer, people come to this place mainly to dig clams. On a good day of a minus tide, more than 30,000 diggers will flock to the beaches to hunt the elusive razor clam.

In late autumn and winter, only a few resorts stay open to accommodate the few people who enjoy the quiet solitude of the season and the noisy violence of a wintry sea. This is the beachcombers' season. The peninsula catches huge amounts of drift from the Japanese current in winter, most of it snaffled off the beach by professionals before it comes firmly to rest. The trick is to get up and follow the incoming highest high tide of the day, working along the edge of the advancing surf. One professional, using a car, set what is probably the world's free-style record for collecting Japanese glass fishing floats. He got 220 of them on one tide in 1963, a high tide that came on the heels of a storm. (As a matter of fact, professionals comb almost every coast on the beach this way. Amateurs have to work professional hours, or take slim leavings, or buy something along the road.) It is not wise for an amateur to drive a car on a beach at night. Two people walking together with good flashlights can cover a lot of beach and have a fine time at it.

If looking for drift palls, the dawn hours can be productive of a mess of fresh Dungeness crab. Crabs often gather in the troughs between sand bars, and always a few get caught in pools left by the ebbing tides (these are the "crab holes" local people talk about). They can be caught bare-handed or with a crab rake. The best-known crab holes on the peninsula are north of the beach road at Ocean Park, and in the area just north of Beard's Hollow. This kind of crabbing is done near strong rip currents, and needs to be approached with caution.

**Leadbetter State Park** occupies the northerly tip of the peninsula, an eerie desert of sand dunes, scrub growth,

*Calm autumn afternoon at Nahcotta's oyster harbor*

*Drift hunter's beach at Bush Pacific Pioneer Park*

small animal tracks and contrasting shores. It fronts on both ocean and bay.

To this point, it is undeveloped. It takes good physical endurance to get anywhere in the soft, shifting mounds of sand. For the dedicated naturalist, loner, or hunter for little-dug clam beds, it is at least potentially worth a trip down a road that gets more and more extemporaneous as it proceeds.

As far as Oysterville, the road is two wide lanes of macadam. Once beyond that tiny settlement (heading west), a spur road turns north. It is graded dirt for a while, then becomes ungraded dirt, and finally proceeds the last two miles as a wagon track. It ends, mysteriously, at a pair of concrete slabs. Some local people remember this as a one-time coast guard station. Others recall that is was a small oyster cannery. Several remember, with more certainty, that this was once the tip of the peninsula. Now, it is more than half a mile west from the slabs to the shore, and a good deal more than a mile north to the tip of the park and harbor mouth.

### OYSTER TOWNS

Two small oyster towns huddle on the shore of Willapa Bay. They offer little to the activist, but are worthy of visit by observers of rare industries, and photographers and water colorists who think highly of aging and picturesque architecture, both residential and marine. The names of the towns are **Nahcotta** and **Oysterville,** and they can be reached directly from Ilwaco via Peninsula Road, or through Long Beach to Ocean Park, then east a few blocks.

The canneries and smoke houses welcome visitors in season. Late fall and early winter is the active time. Summers, there is very little fishing, and therefore very little processing.

The waters of the bay are almost always placid, and herons stalk the shoreline from time to time. Anybody who has a boat can cross to Long Island in the south tip of the bay, and dig littlenecks (rock cockles) for steaming. There are no boat launches, so the easy way is just to buy a bucket of them already steamed at a shoreside restaurant.

## Willapa Bay

Far the greater part of this bay's shore is unsuited to beach walking. Much of it is fringed by swampy ground or out and out bogs. The tide zone is mainly mudflats, the fact that makes the oyster farm a possibility. The towns of South Bend and Raymond are all business. Their shores are devoted entirely to harbor facilities for the lumber and oyster industries. Still, rimmed by fir-covered, rolling hills, the bay is pleasant to see. The drive around it has moments of genuine beauty, and the two parks that give access to the shore are pleasant places to while away an hour or a day.

**Bush Pacific Pioneer Park** and the adjoining oyster town of **Bay Center** are 15 miles west of Raymond, on a point two miles west of U.S. 101. The spur road cuts west across a marsh full of red-winged blackbirds from a point just at the south end of the Palix River bridge.

Bay Center comes first, a random collection of piers and frame buildings surrounded by metal tubs, wire baskets, and other tools of the oystering trade. The business area lies in the lee of a rounded hill, atop which are the homes of the town residents and the state park.

The park has two parts. The top of the hill is mainly an open-floored stand of tall fir with picnic sites scattered about in dappled shade and on a unique duff made up of

*Foreign freighter unloads oyster spat at Raymond*

equal parts of fir needles and oyster shells. A rudimentary baseball diamond takes up the greater part of a small clearing just inside the gate.

The other part of the park is its shore, an unusual shore in matters of appearance. It has offshore protuberances that look faintly like seastacks, but are of a very soft and warm-hued sandstone. At the north end of the park shore, a welter of anciently downed trees have been worn into surrealist sculptures by the gentle lap of bay waves. Everywhere offshore are oyster beds, and also beds of jackknife and butter clams. At almost any time of year, this is a sparsely populated park beach (partly because the bay bottom here is full of snags and no good at all for swimming).

**Bruceport Park,** a Pacific County park, commemorates the site of the original oystering community on this bay. It is five miles north of the Palix River, and, like Bush Pacific Park, crowns a small, rounded hill. Its primary use is as a picnic park, with its sites overlooking the tranquil view.

From either of these parks it is possible in spring or late fall to watch the oystermen working their beds with boats or scows.

**Raymond** and **South Bend,** if not shore-oriented, are the best headquarters for exploring the margins of the bay on a weekend. They are also the best place to see oyster spat being loaded from freighters onto the scows of local oystermen.

North and west of these side-by-side towns, Washington State Highway 105 stays close to the bay all the way out to Tokeland, on the north spit. It is a scenic route, straight and wide, and it leads to an oft-overlooked stretch of Pacific shoreline between the mouths of Grays Harbor bay and Willapa bay. The reasons for going there are outlined in the succeeding section.

## A short history of oysters

In a small but just irony, one of the world's worst cooks was responsible for starting the commercial farming of oysters in Willapa Bay.

During December, 1851, the schooner *Robert Bruce* lay at anchor in the bay while its crew gathered newly-found oysters, to be sold to San Francisco restaurants. The men passed much of their spare time grousing about the villainous meals they got. The cook, a man with no taste for criticism, responded by drugging all his mates and firing the ship. Local Indians saved the seamen while the cook escaped and the *Bruce* burned to the waterline.

With nothing else to do and nowhere to go, the erstwhile mariners turned to harvesting the shellfish and selling them to other ships in the oyster trade. Their original headquarters was Bruceport, a town since abandoned and now marked only by a sign on U.S. 101. Oysterville and Nahcotta on the North Beach Peninsula, and Bay Center 15 miles south of Raymond and two miles west of U.S. 101 are the home ports for oystermen working the south end of the bay. Tokeland and South Bend harbor fleets that work the north loop of the bay.

The original farmers exhausted the supply of native oysters, which were closely related to the Olympias now found only in Hood Canal and adjacent waters. The present-day oystermen in Willpap Bay farm the Pacific Oyster (*Crassostrea gigas*), a bigger and moodier creature. The natives reproduced regularly, but the Pacific oyster has a history of inattention to this requirement in these waters. Because of this, most of the young (called spat) are imports of Japanese or Canadian parentage. Freighters call at Raymond, mainly in April, to unload strings of old oyster shells to which clusters of spat are attached.

These strings, called cultch, are barged to the beds, where they are attached to the cross-pieces of the curious picket fences that mark all such beds. The spat mature into very young oysters thus suspended, after which the old shells are unstrung and cast onto the muddy sand of the beds. A year later, men go out into the beds with spikes to shatter the old host shells, freeing each cluster of young oysters to grow unhampered.

When the animals are mature and ready for harvest, they are either dredged off the bottom, or are picked by hand. The harvest usually starts in late September, after the water has cooled enough for the oysters to become firm-fleshed after the spawning season (which falls mainly in the months without R's in them). The hand-harvest has a certain charm. Workers carry big wire baskets at low tide into the beds, where pre-positioned barges rest in strategic locations. Bigger metal tubs are sometimes used. In either case, the pickers work around the barges, collecting the animals by the hundreds.

Commercial oyster farming is also carried on in Grays Harbor (Washington), Tillamook Bay, Yaquina Bay, Coos Bay, and Netarts Bay (Oregon), and Tomales Bay and Drake's Estero (California).

The beds are almost all private ones, and public picking is not allowed. But in almost all cases the oystermen sell fresh oysters by the roadsides. The one exception is the Nema Reserve in Willapa Bay, north of Bay Center.

# Rugged Olympic Peninsula

It is traditional among Washingtonians to "make The Loop" at any reasonable opportunity. The Loop is U.S. 101 from Olympia around the perimeter of the Olympic Peninsula to Grays Harbor, then back to Olympia on U.S. 410.

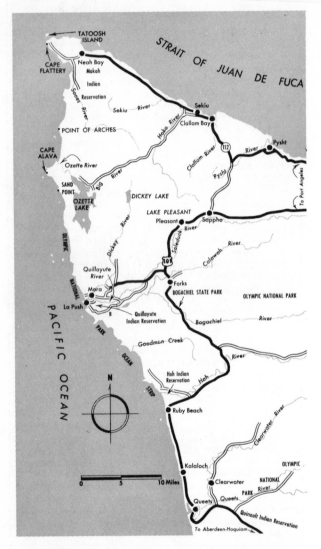

**SHORESIDE CAMPING:** *Olympic National Park campgrounds at Lake Ozette, Ericson Bay (on Lake Ozette), Mora (across river from LaPush), Kalaloch. Ocean City State Park (north spit of Grays Harbor) (153 units, 29 trailer units); Twin Harbors State Park (south of Westport) (370 units, 49 trailer units).* **SHORESIDE ACCOMMODATIONS:** *At Port Angeles, Crescent Beach, Clallam Bay, Sekiu, Neah Bay, Lake Ozette, LaPush, Kalaloch, Queets, Moclips, Pacific Beach, Copalis Beach, Ocean City, Ocean Shores. Inshore accommodations at Aberdeen, Hoquiam. Write for Olympic Peninsula Resort and Hotel Association list, c/o Port Angeles C of C, 1217 East First Street, Port Angeles. Westport and Grayland have many motels at or near the shore. No list is available.*

The highway distance is not much, about 320 miles. But it can take weeks to poke into the numberless crannies of Puget Sound, a Victorian relic of a town at Port Townsend, some awesome mountains, and some equally awesome seacoast. For the shore-oriented, fishing, clamming, rock-hounding, tidepooling, skin diving, driftwood hunting, and beach hiking are rewarding diversions.

The ocean shore of the northwest corner of Washington distinguishes itself by several qualities. Its rocky, forested headlands possess a brooding beauty in these rainy latitudes. The waters offshore are rich in salmon. The beaches are rich in clams, mussels, and other edibles. Several Indian communities are largely intact, places to see rare, ancient skills in current use.

But it is the absence of any kind of road from more than 20 miles of a generally unpopulated shoreline that most distinctly sets this region apart from other lengths of Pacific shore. The greater part of the distance falls within the boundaries of the Olympic National Park seashore strip, where conservationists hope it is immune to human improvement, so later generations can come to make an arduous walk to see how the land was when the first Europeans saw it.

## The Northwest Corner

In Washington the Pacific Ocean ends or begins, depending on which way the observer is headed, at Tongue Point 16 miles west of Port Angeles. Science says that the "littoral line of the Pacific Coast" ends there, and that the 66 miles of shoreline west along the Strait of Juan de Fuca is general tidal shoreline. Once around the tip of Cape Flattery, it requires no scientist's judgment to know that it is indeed ocean hammering ashore.

### THE STRAIT OF JUAN DE FUCA

The primary allure of the area is for deep-water salmon fishermen, who put out from Port Angeles, a private park at Agate Beach, Sekiu, and Neah Bay. Some of the beaches are suited to hiking, swimming, and clamming.

**Agate** and **Crescent Beach Park** is an unusually large private development for boaters and campers. Agate Beach is especially rich in rocks scoured out of other earth and deposited here by glaciers of the last Ice Age.

While the private property is extensive, some nearby government holdings can be reached with minor effort either by walking along the beach, or by poking about on county roads leading north off State 112.

Tongue Point is at the east end of these adjacent beaches (Crescent is the easterly one). It is, in addition to being the end of the ocean, the site of a marker noting boundary agreements of 1908 between the United States and Canada.

A road at Joyce, 16 miles west of Port Angeles, leads to the private park entrance on a point between the two beaches. The government holdings, in **Salt Creek Recreation Area,** are to the west of this park.

**Whiskey Creek Beach,** three miles west of Joyce, is

*Clammers work Ruby Beach in Olympic National Park. Highway is conveniently very near beach at this point*

another private campground giving access to long expanses of rocky shore.

**Pillar Point,** at the mouth of the Pysht River 40 miles west of Port Angeles, has a considerable beach area in public use. There is a welter of names surrounding the place. It is called Butler's Cove County Park on some maps, the Merrill and Ring Recreation Area on others, and merely Pysht on still others.

The county maintains a boat launch. Otherwise, the 1,000 acres of forested headland and gravelly cove is not much developed. As is the case with the other beaches along the Strait, rockhounding is a primary attraction with skin-diving (mainly for octopus) a close second among the more or less shorebound. Salmon draw far greater numbers.

**Clallam Bay** and **Sekiu,** a pair of sportfishing towns, mark the point where State 112 rejoins the shore (it runs inland after Pysht). The towns have little other purpose than as harbors for private, rental, and charter boats, but they are situated on some handsome shoreline.

**Hoko Beach** lies just west of Sekiu, between the mouths of the Hoko River and Sekiu River and extending west beyond the latter stream. The land is owned by a timber company, but the trees on it are for the moment marginal. The active logging is not intense, and the shore is heavily used by beachcombers, rockhounds, tidepoolers, skin divers and steelhead fishermen (both streams have good runs).

The beach, rimmed tightly by trees, never exceeds more than 30 yards in width, although the woods are somewhat penetrable for a short distance from the shore.

## CAPE FLATTERY

The Cape itself is wondrously rugged and hard to use. Most of the area considered to be "cape" is also the reservation of the Makah Indians, who operate a considerable sportfishing harbor for salmon just on the strait side of the tip of the cape.

**Neah Bay** is the town and salmon harbor. It is the end of State 112, and the Makah tribal headquarters. Like Sekiu and Clallam Bay it has motels, cottages, stores, and the other trappings of a resort town.

The roads beyond it are not engineered to modern standards, but four-wheel-drive vehicles and walkers can penetrate to some scenic beaches.

**Cape Flattery** requires hard work to see. The road is not much good once beyond the Makah Air Force Station. Experienced backwoods drivers can penetrate a certain distance. Beyond that, it is more intriguing to hike anyway. Spur roads head off to the edges of sheer rock walls deeply pocked by wave action, or to abandoned artillery bunkers.

It is possible to get down to the water's edge at certain places on low tides, but getting caught by a high tide can be fatal. The low tide rewards are some outstanding marine gardens.

*Frothy seawater teases walker on Shi-Shi Beach*

*The shape of the rocks gives Cannonball Beach its name*

The main road (or trail) persists all the way to the tip of the point, to Look-Through Rock, from where Tatoosh Island and the light station are visible.

**Mukkaw Bay** runs south from the cape to Portage Head. It is within the Makah reservation, and entirely undeveloped. However, the hardy are permitted to camp in the narrow meadow behind the shore if they wish. The road to it forks south near the Air Force station and continues in some degree as far as Shi-Shi Beach south of Portage Head.

**Shi-Shi Beach** is reached by the next best thing to no road at all. In fact, most modern cars cannot penetrate much farther than Portage Head (where an abandoned bus serves as a dandy marker ) and even that distance is a severe test of shocks and springs. Shi-Shi Beach is 158 miles west of Port Angeles, and a good 30 miles beyond State 112's intersection with a tie-road to U.S. 101. It takes a firm commitment to spend a day nosing about before a passer-through can get all the way out to the beach, which is a serene three-mile crescent of sand between Portage Head and Point of the Arches. Offshore, rocks churn the surf into a white froth that is fine to see at any time, but this is mainly a low tide beach. Tidepoolers delight in it then, and beachwalkers can explore wave-cut arches and sea tunnels dry-footed and fearless.

Along with the abundant life of the tidepools there is non-marine animation in the tangled forest that comes right down to the driftwood line. The most dramatic of these is the bald eagle. There are several nests in the tall snags' tops, and the sharp-eyed can sometimes see the huge birds flying low above the surf line, well out over the water.

It is impossible to walk the beach around Point of the Arches, or to clamber over that brush-choked headland to get to the ocean strip of Olympic National Park. That takes backtracking at least as far as Sekiu.

# Olympic National Park

The Olympic Strip of the Olympic National Park is hardly a quarter of a mile wide in some places, but it is more than 30 miles long and it has very little in the way of roads. It is this last fact that makes it a favored haunt of beach hikers, tidepool explorers, and seekers after the remotest kind of solitude accessible on the United States' Pacific Ocean shore.

## CAPE ALAVA AND LAKE OZETTE

The only access to the shore in the 25 miles of coast between road's end at Neah Bay and road's end at LaPush is by trail from Lake Ozette.

The lake is one of the largest in the state. Its east shore is being logged, and its west shore is safe within the park, which creates the kind of impression offered by a man half way through a haircut. The standing forest is so thick, however, that the scars of the east side can be ignored easily.

There is a resort at the north tip of the lake, where the 22-mile road from Sekiu ends. Across the Ozette River from the resort is a National Park Service campground. From one place or the other it is possible to launch a beach hike of almost any length on one of four trails.

**Cape Alava,** the westernmost point in the 48 connected states, lies at the end of one of the trails three and one-third miles from the resort. The trail is typical of all of them, muddy but easy walking through moss-festooned forest carpeted with ferns, salal, dwarf dogwood and young trees spouting from the remains of fallen giants. Small meadows occur. The roar of the surf is audible for a long time, but the ocean remains hidden from a walker's view until he steps out of the forest above the back edge of the beach.

Once at this picturesque point, site of an abandoned village, it is possible to head either north or south along the beach.

North a mile is Cannonball Island (also called Indian Island), the name of which comes from the large spherical concretions that wash out of its steep side. The island lends itself to exploration at low tide, but getting trapped on it means sitting out a six hour tide change.

Is is possible to walk the now sandy now rocky beach five miles, to the south side of Point of the Arches. About a mile north of Cannonball Island is Carson Sea Cave, an impressive marine garden of plants and animals. It can be rounded only at low tide. Just beyond it the mouth of the Ozette River cannot be forded in all seasons, but is sometimes passable in summer.

Within this distance, hikers at low tide will come across bits of pieces of the bark *Austria*, wrecked in 1887. Her anchor is the most noticeable remnant, but there are some pieces of hull, and a bollard and some chain. She was a good vessel, 18 years old, 1,300 tons, and in able hands when a gale blew her ashore. No lives were lost in the wreck and she went largely unmourned.

Matters did not go so well for three other ships that came to bad ends along this shore. Memorials mark the sites of their tragic wrecks farther south.

**Sand Point** is at the end of a three-mile trail that runs southwest from the Lake Ozette Campground, and runs onto the beach three miles south of Cape Alava.

It is an uncomplicated nine-mile hike down this trail, north along the beach, then back up to the Cape Alava Trail to the resort. Heading south from Sand Point means timing the stroll to get around one or more points on medium low tides. It is no walk for a novice, but not hazardous to go all the way to LaPush, 16 miles south.

Going to that effort will take a walker past the memorials to shipwrecks noted above.

The first of these, the Norwegian Memorial, is roughly even with the south tip of Lake Ozette, about eight miles south of Sand Point. The dedicated beach hiker will find the shore rewarding for scenery, tidepools, the possible sight of a wild animal scouting the water's edge for food (most likely late in the day or very early), and for the guaranteed exertion of scrambling up and over one or more of the small points along the shore. Another, far easier way is to rent a boat ride from the Lake Ozette Resort to Allen's Bay, from where a two-plus mile trail drops to the shore exactly at the Norwegian Memorial.

The Chilean Memorial is five miles on south of the Norwegian, just around the tip of Cape Johnson, or just three miles up the beach from LaPush, where a spur road from U.S. 101 ends just short of the shore.

The Norwegian Memorial marks the common grave of

## Northwest surf fishing

Surf fishing in the salmon-oriented Northwest comes as a discovery to many fishing families. Salmon trolling may be more spectacular, yet surf fishing combines a number of enjoyable elements with inexpensiveness.

It is license-free, and the catch limits are generous. The states close very few areas. The open beaches stay open the year around. Also, good clamming tides are good fishing tides, so one weekend outing can cover both bases.

In the waters north of Point Conception, the predominant fish are surfperch, flounder, ling cod, true cod, greenlings, and sablefish. Halibut crop up in the surf zone sometimes, but tend to stay in deeper water.

The best conditions occur during the last three hours of flood tide and the first three hours of ebb tide. Sportfish come close to shore in pursuit of baitfish. Surfperch and flounder feed on mollusks and crustaceans covered by high tide waters. Greatest activity of fish (and so fishermen) comes with the spring tides, at full moon, and new moon.

Flounder often lie at the bottom of deep holes inshore of a sandbar, and are best taken by casting across the hole and retrieving through the deep water.

A number of these fish seem to feed along the shelves of beaches that have abrupt drop-offs just out from shore. On ebb tides, the mouths of tidal streams and inlets may be productive as baitfish retreat down them with the tide. The usual technique with these is to cast from the downstream side of the "set" into the deepest part of the channel.

In the rockier and less regular stretches of the northern California and northwest coasts, short beaches flanked at either side by rocky headlands offer an admixture of surf and rock fishing. The condition prevails generally enough that the versatile 9 to 10-foot fibreglass rod with a 250-foot-capacity, level-wind surf reel does the most effective job. A mixed bag of artificial lures and food baits are in the gear of most veteran anglers. Big wobbling spoons seem to work well for black rockfish and ling cod. Surfperch seem partial to sand worms and razor clams. The line is usually a 12-pound test monofilament.

Some of Washington's most fished beaches are Neah Bay, LaPush, Kalaloch, the whole string of beaches from Moclips to Ocean Shores, Westport, and the North Beach Peninsula (especially near the Columbia mouth). In Oregon, the south jetty area of the Columbia, the south spit of Tillamook Bay, Bastendorff Beach near Coos Bay and Bandon get heavy action. Californians work the sandy beaches of Sonoma and Marin counties, the whole shore from San Francisco to Santa Cruz, and Monterey Bay.

*Olympic National Park has mile after mile of driftwood strewn beaches . . . collectors don't even dent the supply*

*Beach Hikers at Hole-in-the-wall north of Rialto*

18 men who perished in the wreck of the three-masted bark *Prince Arthur*, which mistook a cabin's light for that of Tatoosh Island and turned into the rocks on a January night in 1903.

The Chilean Memorial marks the final resting place of the schooner *W. J. Pirrie* and 20 of the 22 aboard when she ran aground in November, 1920. (She followed another Chilean vessel ashore on this point by some 37 years, a bark named the *Lenore* having grounded with lives lost on the earlier date.)

## RIALTO BEACH AND LaPUSH

A dirt road of rather good quality turns west from U.S. 101 about a mile north of the town of Forks, and pursues a scenic way toward the sea. Six miles before it gets there, the motorist has a last chance to choose between Rialto Beach on the north side of the Quillayute River and La-Push on the south side of it.

**Rialto Beach** is a center of national park activity in this coastal strip. There is a campground and ranger station at Mora, well inshore along the river, and there is a picnic ground at the end of the road, right next to the beach. The beach is broad and sandy, and the site of a particularly good smelt run. LaPush is visible across the river, James Island is accessible to waders at low tide, and a hike up the beach toward Cape Johnson is complicated only by the mouths of two small creeks, each easier to ford at low tide than high, and the arch at one of them open to passage only at low tide.

**LaPush,** on the south side of the River, is a salmon harbor (commercial and sport) in the Quillayute Indian Reservation, and a resort of long standing on the Washing-

*Several varieties* of kelp litter the beach, attracting the interest of visitors from inner and outer space

ton coast. (The Indian residents of the town have retained their traditional skill with the dugout canoe while running efficient modern resort businesses.) Three beaches string out along the shore south of the town, all easily accessible. Beyond those beaches, the coast reaches what many think is its scenic peak, and some of the most difficult terrain for beach hikers.

First Beach adjoins the south jetty of the Quillayute in LaPush. It has its own parking lot, on the back side of a tremendous tangle of driftwood. The south end of it is marked by a small sea cave that is, most of the time, home to a quantity of starfish. The cave, a reasonably photogenic one, takes less effort to reach than almost any other in the national park.

Second Beach can be reached along the shore at low tide, but is handier by way of a trail that joins the road into town. A seastack close inshore and rugged Teahwhit Head to the south make this one of the most scenic beaches in the region. The tidepools along Teahwhit Head are good ones (Ruth Kirk once observed that this is one of the best places in the world to observe intertidal invertebrates because the fog is sometimes so thick that the animals don't notice the tide has gone out and left them behind. Her book, *The Olympic Seashore*, is an indispensable guide to serious explorers and a charmingly literate companion for every visitor to take along. It is published by the Olympic Natural History Association at $1.95.)

Third Beach is accessible only by trail from the LaPush Road. Teahwhit Head cannot be rounded safely or climbed at all. From a point near the south end of this beach begins the long and difficult trail to Oil City, 14 miles south. Hikers must clamber over several lofty headlands, slither along on seaweed-slicked boulders. Once arrived at Oil City

*At low tide* beachwalkers round Cape Johnson

*Tidepool browsers in Olympic National Park*

*Sea stack at LaPush dwarfs beach stroller*

(which is a name and no more than that), the hiker is 12 gravel-road-miles from U.S. 101 and without any choice but going that way.

### RUBY BEACH TO QUEETS

U.S. 101 joins the shore at Ruby Beach, the first presence of a highway near the water south of Cape Flattery. It stays along the shore to the end of the park south of Kalaloch, then turns inland again to skirt around the Quinault Indian Reservation.

The beaches are numbered consecutively from #1 south of Kalaloch to Beach #7, a little more than two miles south of Ruby Beach. Kalaloch is the site of a lodge and ranger station and a national park campground.

This stretch is, as the superficial evidence would indicate, the easiest part of the national park shore to get to, and to move around in. Each of the beaches has some distinguishing characteristic. Beach #1 has a genuine shingle, #2 has drift logs by the hundreds, #6 has a shipwreck. The trails are all less than a half-mile, and few of them are much more than a tenth.

Kalaloch Beach has razor clam beds and Beach #4 is noted for its smelt run. Surf fishing is likely to be good anywhere along the strip.

# The North Beaches

The north in the name comes from the geographic relationship to Aberdeen and Hoquiam on Grays Harbor. For a long time the good citizens of these side-by-side lumber and fishing towns had the North Beaches pretty much to themselves. In mobile modern times as many as 30,000 visitors filter through the towns on their way to dig razor clams on a favorable tide.

The shore is served by a stub road, Washington State Highway 109, which ambles its crooked way 41 miles from Hoquiam to Taholah, where it ceases. Wherever a stretch of flat sand beach makes a good environment for razor clams there is a resort or a town full.

**Ocean Shores** is a town full, is in fact an enormous resort full of restaurants, motels, homesites, art galleries, a golf course, and every other kind of firm that might expect to give aid and comfort to a vacationer. It even has car washes especially designed to get salt off the undersides of autos driven along the surf line. The resort is on a spur road, south off State 109. It covers much of the north spit of Grays Harbor, and its ocean shore is a fine razor clam bed.

**Oyehut** is a quieter and smaller extension of the area just north of the main complex of buildings.

**Ocean City State Park** is on the same spur road that goes to Ocean Shores, but its entrance is only a few hundred feet from the junction with State 109. The park spreads out across low, rolling dunes. Most of the campsite area is fairly well sheltered in scrub trees well back from the shore. One road goes west to the shore, where, as is the case all along, razor clams draw hundreds of hardy diggers on the least of days and thousands on the best.

There are good picnic facilities in this park, virtually the only formal ones for miles around (this being the only park in the area).

**Ocean City** on the state highway just north of the park, is the first of a series of similar towns. Each has a store or two, gas stations, motels and trailer parks, and a clam beach.

**Copalis Beach** is one of the oldest and best-known of these towns, and the largest of the lot.

**Pacific Beach,** another eight miles along the road, is somewhat more dramatically set than its neighbors to the south. The road begins to twist and turn across steepening cliffs north of Copalis. The shore begins to be rocky. Pacific Beach is tucked in the lee of a bluff and at the back of a deep cove of sand. The south end is pinched off by a forested

*Old Westport Light overlooks miles of sandy beach*

*Pacific Beach has rich supply of shells, sand dollars*

point, but around the corner to the north stretches a long, narrow ribbon of dark, fine sand that can be walked all the way to Point Grenville Light (open to visitors weekends from 1 to 3 p.m.). In summer, the beach is heavily used by clammers, but in fall it is fair deserted, and huge numbers of sand dollar and snail shells begin to wash up with each tide. There is eight miles of it north to the light station, but clamming is permitted only as far as Moclips. The Quinault Indians reserve the right to their clam beaches.

**Moclips,** on the edge of the reservation, is the last town in the string with tourist facilities. Taholah, inside the reservation, has none. (There is a steady diminution, each succeeding town to the north being smaller than its immediate predecessor.)

All along this part of the coast, beachcombing for Japanese glass fishing floats and other drift is notably rewarding to the persistent. Amateurs have to compete with professionals, but the crop is rich enough for both.

# South of Grays Harbor

Like Willapa Harbor to the south, Grays Harbor has a marshy shore around most of its perimeter, and where it is not marshy it is piers and mills.

South of the harbor, not quite Olympic Peninsula and not quite Southwest Washington, is a short strip of coast that connects the two harbor mouths. It probably would not be much visited if it were not the site of a salmon harbor next to prodigious waters, and also some of the best clam beach along the coast.

**Westport** is the salmon harbor, both commercial and sport, and it has grown at an almost incredible pace. It was a sleepy village in the mid-1950's, with a small fleet of charter boats for sport fishermen and a more sizable fleet of commercial vessels. A couple of restaurants and a motel or two housed a steady stream of visitors in season. Now

the port area has expanded to row after row of finger piers, and there are rows upon rows of motels, hotels, and restaurants to go with them. Sports fishermen put out in such numbers that they annually catch more than 175,000 salmon between April and October (Silvers and Kings as local nomenclature has it).

Immediately to the south, the charms are a bit quieter.

**Twin Harbors State Park** just south of Westport on State 105, is a narrow strip in the sand dunes, with campsites all tight together in a narrow band of scrub trees. Fishermen and clammers compete for the space all summer. This beach, like those north and south, is of fine sand so compact, it can be driven upon. It is one of the good razor clam beds in the state.

**Grayland,** five miles south of the park, is in the main a compound of beach resorts. Its distinguishing feature is a Beachcomber's Derby, held each year just after St. Patrick's Day. Anything collected off the beach between New Year's Day and Saint Paddy's Day is eligible for entry, and most of the drift usually shows up on the judging tables. (Simultaneously there is a more elegant competition for driftwood arrangements.)

Between the state park and Grayland, the road comes close to the back shore of a small cove. In summer, a lagoon builds in the sand, and this sun-warmed water is a fine place to swim on the Fourth of July or any other sunny, summery day. In winter, the hunting of Japanese glass fishing floats (anywhere on the Washington coast is a good place but this is as good as any) or other drift is a more sensible thing to do.

**Tokeland,** just inside the north spit of Willapa Harbor, is another sportfishing headquarters, although a far smaller one than Westport. There are some oysters on public tideflats in the neighborhood, but it is only wise to make careful local inquiry. The outer side of the north spit is a driftwood hunter's paradise because the road stops well short of the end of it while the currents do not.

# The fun of shell collecting

Along the tideline of any sandy beach, a few seashells nestle in drying kelp or under driftwood. Many of them are ordinary in appearance, dully-colored snail shells. Others are in bright colors and unusual shapes. Almost every beachwalker who comes along yields to the temptation to pick up a few of the fanciful ones.

Some of the people who keep those first randomly gathered shells eventually find themselves lured into trying to gather representatives of each of the 5,000 species found on the Pacific shore from Alaska to Panama, and as many as possible of the 70,000 recorded species in the great world-wide family Mollusca.

Most serious collectors tend to specialize in one of two directions. Conchologists collect shells for their own value. Malacologists interest themselves in the living animals. They study habits in general, and are interested in the shell only incidentally as it reflects the nature of its architect.

A conchologist has the easier lot in that he kills the animal immediately, sparing himself the difficult task of trying to keep alive a delicate mechanism attuned to a highly specific environment. His task is to preserve the delicate beauty and fine detail of the shell so it can be displayed. The malacologist either has to stay where the mollusk lives, or get it into a seawater aquarium that duplicates the natural home of the creature.

For the shore side of the collecting story, see page 37.

Here is a primer on identifying and preparing shells for display.

Conventionally, mollusks are grouped in five major classes:

Gastropods (stomach footed): Snails, which live on land, and in fresh and salt water. In the sea, some live in the tide zone, others below it.

Pelecypods (hatchet footed): Clams, which include both fresh and salt water species. The remaining three classes are found only in sea water.

Amphineura (nerves on both sides): Chitons.

Scaphopods (bowl footed): Tusk shells.

Cephalopods (head footed): Squid, octopus, argonaut and nautilus. In this class are the largest, the most highly developed, the most intelligent of mollusks.

Snails and clams are far and away the most numerous of these classes, and the ones a collector finds first, but all shells can be treated similarly. Several methods adapt to time, distance from home, and equipment at hand.

Sometimes the conchologist far from home simply dumps all but the smallest of his shells into tanks of alcohol to preserve them until he returns to home base and better cleaning facilities. (Most experts are against formalin for this purpose, because the acid that forms as it breaks down will eat away the delicate sculpture of shells, and will in time dissolve some shells completely.) Use isopropyl alcohol, with a little soda added to keep the alcohol neutral as the decaying animal exudes acid.

Once the animals are where they are to be cleaned, either in their alcohol jars or brought alive from nearby beaches, they can be immersed in hot water or frozen.

Hot water is the first choice of many collectors. Treat live shells the first day, if possible, with this method.

Delicate molluscan tissues disintegrate rapidly, and become difficult to extract from their shells.

If the shells brought from a nearby beach have to be left overnight, put them in a covering bath of fresh water.

The cleaning bath should start with cold water covering all the shells completely. The temperature should be raised slowly to 176°F (80°C), and held there until clam shells gape open. The time usually ranges between five and twenty minutes. The water should never come to a boil since boiling causes shells to check and discolor, and causes the flesh of snails especially to become brittle and hard to remove.

Once the shells are cool, clam flesh can be scooped easily from the gaping shell. The shells can be bound shut with thread or propped open while drying; thereafter the ligament will stay stiffly in the pre-set position.

Snails are something else. The flesh has to be coaxed out with a wire hook, an ice pick, or a large pin. Patience is the key. A steady gentle pressure exerted until the last whorl of the animal slips free of the shell is the best bet. Should the animal split in two, there are two ways to retrieve the situation. One is to cup the shell in one hand, with the mouth down, and jar the hand against a solid surface. If that does not cause the stuck piece to pop out, bury the shell in clean sand and let the flesh rot. Neutralize lingering odor with a drop of anise oil or clove oil on a tuft of cotton wadded into the cavity.

Some snails have a horny, trap door-like covering on the foot. When they withdraw into the shell this operculum (Latin for lid) fits over the mouth to form a protective barrier. This should be cut away and saved before the animal is placed in the hot water bath.

Freezing works as well in most cases, better in some, and not so well as hot water in a few. In this case, the shells are placed in a covered plastic container and frozen for 24 hours, then removed to the refrigerator compartment for several days. Freezing kills the animal and breaks down its muscle fibers. During refrigeration, the flesh tends to pull away from the shell, and softens.

The technique is particularly handy with small snails with narrow-mouthed shells. The freezing tends to make the flesh bulge outside the shell slightly, so it is easier to get at than the shrunken flesh of an animal subjected to the hot water treatment. (Conversely, the large snails such as the moon snail tend to have muscles so large that freezing does not deteriorate them enough.)

Tiny snails can be cleaned simply by burying them in a bed of clean sand (not dirt) and allowing the shell to rot clean.

Once the shell is clean of flesh, it sometimes has to be cleaned of external grime. Much of it will come off with a dull scraper and a stiff brush, at the risk of damage to the shell. Some collectors use bleach and muriatic acid, but this almost always whitens any color in the shell, and eats away some of the shell itself. Hand scraping is the purists' only recourse.

Many shells have a brown, leathery protective outer skin called a periostracum. Intact it looks fine. Worn, it has a shabby appearance that calls for getting rid of it with a weak solution of caustic soda.

Once the shells are clean and dry, they should be guarded against mold, fading, or other decomposition. One way is to rub the shell gently with a solution of

Here and on page 110 we show only a few West Coast shells, chosen to indicate the variety of shells native to our shores. We use scientific names for your reference. Some of the shells have no accepted common name. **1** Conus regularis Sowerby, **2** Conus perplexus Sowerby, **3** Conus ximenes Gray, **4** Pyrene fuscata Sowerby, **5** Cantharus pallidus Broderip and Sowerby, **6** Eupleura muriciformis Broderip, **7** Cardita affinis Sowerby, **8** Malea ringens Swainson, **9** Lima tetrica Gould, **10** Melongena patula Broderip and Sowerby, **11** Oliva spirata Bolten, **12** Turbo fluctuosus Wood, **13** Donax punctatos-triatus Hanley, **14** Natica chemnitzi Pfeiffer, **15** Ficus decussata Wood, **16** Pitar lupanaria Lesson, **17 & 18** Cypraea cervinetta Kiener, **19** Polinices helicoides Gray, **20** Tellina simulans C. B. Adams, **21** Pecten circularis Sowerby, **22** Cardium procerum Sowerby, **23** Chione californiensis Broderip, **24** Dosinia dunkeri Philippi, **25** Pinna rugosa Sowerby, **26** Purpura patula pansa Gould, **27** Astraea unguis Wood, **28** Solen rosaceus Carpenter, **29** Pecten subnodosus Sowerby, **30** Ostrea corteziana Hertlein, **31** Jenneria pustulata Solander, **32** Agaronia testacea Lamarck, **33** Amiantis callosa Conrad

equal parts of glycerine, isopropyl alcohol, and water.

After the shell dries with its sealer coat on it, it should be labeled and placed in a display box or case. (Snails with an operculum should have that piece glued to a tuft of cotton and the cotton wadded into the shell to hold it in place to aid in specific identifications.) Serious collectors do not glue shells down because they are then lost forever as trade bait in a growing, changing collection.

Identification depends on a good handbook. The idea of learning Latin names boggles some apprentice collectors, but it isn't all that difficult. The Latin names have genuine meaning; the same words crop up over and over again. If that doesn't clinch the argument, the great majority of the world's mollusks do not have any other than their Latin names.

Four good books: *How to Know the American Marine Shells* by R. Tucker Abbott (Signet Key Book KT 375, New York, 1961, 75 cents); *Sea Shells of the World* by R. Tucker Abbott and H. Zim (Golden Press, New York, 1962, $1); *Pacific Sea-Shells* by Spencer W. Tinker (Charles E. Tuttle Co., Rutland, Vt., 1958, $3.25) concentrates on Hawaii; and *West Coast Shells* by Josiah Keep and Joshua L. Baily (Stanford Press, 1935) out of print, but in libraries and a joy to read.

1 *Megathura crenulata* Sowerby, 2 *Lottia gigantea* Gray, 3 *Crucibulum spinosum* Sowerby, 4 *Crepidula onyx* Sowerby, 5 *Crepidula nummaria* Gould, 6 *Thais lamellosa* Gmelin, 7 *Thais canaliculata compressa* Dall, 8 *Tegula funebrale* A. Adams, 9 *Tegula brunnea* Philippi, 10 *Astraea gibberosa* Dillwyn, 11 *Acmaea pelta* Eschscholtz, 12 *Diodora aspera* Eschscholtz, 13 *Pecten hindsi* Carpenter, 14 *Pecten hericius* Gould, 15 *Olivella biplicata* Sowerby, 16 *Nassarius fossatus* Gould, 17 *Ceratostoma foliatum* Gmelin, 1ª *Conus californicus* Hinds, 19 *Ceratostoma nuttalli* Conrad, 20 & 22 *Calliostoma annulatum* Lightfoot (22 treated with acid), 21 *Ocenebra lurida* Middendorff, 23 *Calliostoma canaliculatum* Lightfoot, 24 *Hinnites multirugosus* Gale, 25 *Pecten monotimeris* Conrad, 26 *Pecten hastatus* Sowerby, 27 *Pecten aequisulcatus* Carpenter, 28 *Stenoplax conspicua* Carpenter, 29 *Cypraea spadicea* Swainson, 30 *Trivia solandri* Gray, 31 *Kellettia kellettii* Forbes, 32 *Forreria belcheri* Hinds, 33 *Apolymetis biangulata* Carpenter, 34 *Pecten diegensis* Hinds, 35 *Cardium nuttallii* Conrad, 36 *Chama pellucida* Broderip, 37 *Bursa californica* Hinds, 38 *Neptunea lirata* Baird, 39 *Fusitriton oregonense* Redfield, 40 *Semele decisa* Conrad, 41 *Pododesmus cepio* Gray, 42 *Tivela stultorum* Mawe, 43 *Modiolus capax* Conrad, 44 *Bulla gouldiana* Pilsbry, 45 *Polinices lewisi* Gould, 46 *Polinices recluziana* Deshayes, 47 *Panope generosa* Gould, 48 *Siliqua patula* Dixon, 49 *Macoma secta* Conrad, 50 *Cardium quadragenarium* Conrad, 51 *Haliotis rufescens* Swainson, 52 *Haliotis cracherodii* Leach, 53 *Haliotis corrugata* Gray

# Index